VISIONS
of
GRANDEUR

VISIONS of GRANDEUR

LEADERSHIP THAT CREATES POSITIVE CHANGE

RALPH T. MATTSON

MOODY PRESS

CHICAGO

Scripture quotations marked (NASB) are taken from the *New American Standard Bible,* © 1960, 1962, 1963, 1968, 1971, 1972, 1973, 1975, and 1977 by The Lockman Foundation, and are used by permission.

Scripture quotations marked (NIV) are taken from *The Holy Bible: New International Version®*. NIV®. Copyright © 1973, 1978, 1984 International Bible Society. Used by permission of Zondervan Publishing House. All rights reserved.

Scripture quotations marked (TLB) are taken from *The Living Bible* © 1971. Used by permission of Tyndale House Publishers, Inc., Wheaton, IL 60189. All rights reserved.

Scripture quotations marked (PHILLIPS) are taken from *The New Testament in Modern English*. Translated by J. B. Phillips. New York: Macmillan, 1958. © J. B. Phillips 1958.

Scripture quotations marked (RSV) are taken from the *The Holy Bible: Revised Standard Version* © 1962, 1973 by Oxford University Press, Inc.

Scripture quotations marked (NEB) are taken from the *New English Bible with the Apocrypha* © 1961, 1970, the Delegates of the Oxford University Press and the Syndics of the Cambridge University.

Scripture quotations marked (KJV) are taken from the King James Version.

The use of selected references from various versions of the Bible in this publication does not necessarily imply publisher endorsement of the versions in their entirety.

The term "praxis" originates from Greek philosophy. It refers to almost any kind of activity a person is likely to perform, in particular, all kinds of business and political activity. It also relates to moral conduct, practical application of knowledge, utilizing common sense, following an established practice, applying an established truth, doing what is right.

ISBN: 0-8024-4640-X

1 3 5 7 9 10 8 6 4 2

Printed in the United States of America

To Carolyn,
an extraordinary person,
and my wife

Contents

HOW TO READ
THIS BOOK
--------⌒◯⌒--------

Each person learns in a different way.

One person likes to start with concepts and then move to applications. Another likes to reverse the process. This book is divided into sections, each of which can, for the most part, stand on its own. For that reason it is possible to read them in any sequence the reader would prefer. However, people are designed for both action and thought. We recommend to readers the discipline of keeping the pragmatics balanced with conceptualization.

Section 1. Thinking. Poses the problem with how we currently think about leaders and their development. Chapters 1–6.

Section 2. Discovery. Introduces styles of leadership and describes how you can discover your leadership gifts. Chapters 7–8.

Section 3. Application to individuals. Deals with how leaders act in practical terms and also in regard to character. Chapters 9–10.

Section 4. Application to organizations. This provides a commentary on what we perceive to be the timely, broad leadership issues in business, churches, schools, and family. Chapters 11–13.

INTRODUCTION

VISIONS OF GRANDEUR

I f we add up all the grand moments of our lives, most of us end with a very small pile of memories, but they are, indeed, golden. In contrast, a similar collection of all our mundane times yields a ponderous heap. It's clear that the bulk of our lives' efforts are consumed by routine tasks and ordinary occasions.

The hope of reversing that imbalance appears in a dream common to many of us. This is a vision of achieving splendid achievements as outstanding, or even famous, leaders. For those already in positions of leadership, the dream may be to somehow redeem what now seems strangely bland. Then for countless others, it is to be part of an organization that is energized by a splendid cause, and that cares about those who do the work.

Hidden behind all those hopes resides the ultimate vision, a vision of genuine grandeur that cannot and will not disappoint. It is a vision that will be achieved because God is the dreamer. Fortunately, we are the actors in that grand play, and He is the creative director. This book considers some of the key players.

Where is your place in this vision?
Why are we so confused about leaders?
What kind of a leader are you?
What kind of organization makes sense for you?
What is leadership in business?
    in churches?
    in schools?
    in families?

As a Christian, I enjoy the diversity God has created, so we will consider corporations as well as churches, business people as well as pastors, management principles as well as theology. God made it all possible, so we expect to discover truth everywhere.

The content of the following is backed up in three ways.

1. The identification of leadership gifts and the assumptions behind them are informed by thousands of cases in our files. They involve people of all ages who found themselves relatively ignorant about what they had to offer the world. They engaged us to assist them in discovering their gifts and in making quality decisions about their lives. As clients, they invariably confirmed the accuracy of the information we provided them. The technology we used in helping them has been recognized by many as being on the cutting edge of what is happening in human resource development.

2. The commentaries on organizations comes from my experience as a leader, plus decades of consulting with key leaders in corporations, professional firms, churches, and schools. Our company, The DOMA Group, has done considerable work in developing leadership teams to effectively complement the president or director. That has provided much insight to the precision needed to tap the otherwise hidden resources of leadership always present in organizations.

3. The conceptual perspectives have emerged out of considerable tangling with the contradictions I find in life and in me. Much probing has borne fruit, but nothing like that of being grasped by God Himself. One can scarcely believe the intensity of what the gospels announce ultimately awaits us, but I know it is reality. That reality informs all our days, ordinary or otherwise. It also enables us to be tough in viewing ourselves, our work, and our organizations.

With gratitude

To Arthur Miller,
coauthor of *Finding a Job You Can Love* and
my first mentor in matters of giftedness

To Chris Ehlers and Robert Sutherland,
comrades-in-arms and supporters of this project

SECTION ONE
RETHINKING LEADERSHIP

He thinks too much: such men are dangerous.

WILLIAM SHAKESPEARE, *Julius Caesar*

Think soberly, according as God hath dealt to every man the measure of faith.

ROMANS 12:3 KJV

CHAPTER 1

─────────⟨⟩─────────

DEFINING
THE LEADER

The most dramatic story of leadership in modern times probably is that of Sir Winston Churchill during the last world war. As Prime Minister, he dragged Britain from its cowering position before the onslaught of the Nazi regime, to take on Adolf Hitler. Realizing the weakness of his nation and seeing the enemy sweeping across all of Europe, Churchill focused the frightened imaginations of his people upon hope and courage.

> You ask, what is our policy?
> I will say: It is to wage war, by sea, land and air
> with all our might and with all the strength God can give us . . .
> That is our policy.
>
> You ask, what is our aim?
> I can answer in one word: It is victory,
> victory at all costs, victory in spite of all terror,
> victory however long and hard the road may be;
> for without victory, there is no survival.[1]

Churchill's story is ideal as a portrayal of how leaders can reverse hopeless situations. The victory Churchill announced was attained in spite of the odds. That reversal is possible everywhere it is needed and in all kinds of organizations, but only if there is appropriate leadership.

Churchill was instrumental in saving an entire nation and ultimately an entire continent because he was the right leader in the right place at the right time. In that place he became the instigator of change; change from despair to hope, change in national readiness, and change from inaction to aggression. This is the product of leadership wherever it appears: change. Every leader is an agent of change. Some leaders bring truth where there is ignorance. Others bring plans and strategies where there is inaction. Where there is purposelessness they bring vision. Where there are needs they initiate help. They make the technical breakthroughs, find the solutions, and bring about creative transformations. All of this denotes change. Change is the common denominator.

The problem with introducing the subject of leadership by using Churchill as an example is that he represents a stature of leadership so high it may diminish our ability to value leadership on all levels, many with only the faintest potential for drama, if any. The issue is not stature, but being in the right place. It is not a matter of fame, but of bringing about sustained progress.

THE OVERWHELMING EVIDENCE OF CHANGE

As we feature the factor of change in defining leadership, we are not presenting it as a value. Those for whom changes are difficult need to understand that. Change is a *condition,* a state of being in which we all live. If we were goldfish it would be the water of our aquarium. As Heraclitus cleverly stated, "Nothing endures but change." If we fail to grasp that we will be unable to appreciate the very nature of leadership.

But why is change primary? Because it is foundational to the nature of existence and of being a person. God created a constantly expanding universe, which means continual change for all that is contained in it, including us. Everything is dynamic, energetic by nature, and it is all moving toward a mysterious culmination in God Himself. This is the ultimate vision of grandeur for mankind as portrayed in the following words by the apostle Paul.

In my opinion whatever we may have to go through now is less than nothing compared with the magnificent future God has planned for us. The whole creation is on tiptoe to see the wonderful sight of the sons of God coming into their own. (*Romans 8:18–19 PHILLIPS*)

CHANGES IN TIME AND SPACE

The dynamics of change permeates every dimension. Time moves us unceasingly toward a future. In space, every galaxy is moving. Every orb within those galaxies moves, including our planet. The earth and everything on it is being thrust through space more than eighteen miles a second, much faster than a speeding bullet.

As we move about our houses we see nothing of these dynamics. We confidently enter rooms we assume are the same spaces we entered yesterday, when in actuality the space that the room was in has passed into far unrecorded distances. We may be in the same place but never in the same space.

Moving away from huge planets to infinitesimal particles of which atoms are composed, we find change again. All particles are in constant motion around the nucleus of each atom. That means that the familiar objects which surround us are constantly changing. They appear to be absolutely stable, but all the particles of which the objects are composed are in different spatial relationships from split second to split second.

Every organism from giraffes to people is moving from its history to the promise of what is ahead. Meanwhile, incredible complexities of organs, cellular structures, and fluid systems are constantly operating to take our bodies with their personalities through time and space, toward their destinies. There is not one particle in the universe that is not going somewhere else. The universe itself is aging. How then can we believe we could nail down anything to prevent it from changing when the nail itself changes from moment to moment?

A living thing is distinguished from a dead thing by the multiplicity of the changes at any moment taking place in it.
Herbert Spencer

CHANGES IN CIVILIZATION

What is true of astronomy, physics, and biology is also true of civilization, our town, our place of work, and our personal futures. However, there is an immense difference between changes in the physical realm and those brought about by human action. The changes in the universe are sovereignly ordained by God's creative will. The changes in civilization are a product of *our* wills, which God sovereignly gave us. The first is a stage for the drama of the second.

The universe gives us time and place to make the millions and millions of decisions and actions that bring about civilization. God has authorized all these decisions, good and bad, over the centuries, and He is exploiting them to ultimately bring about "the sons of God coming into their own."

That is why the most brilliant Christian civilization we know, the medieval, which flourished in Europe from about A.D. 500 to about 1500, believed that *everything* was important. Nothing escaped God's eye, according to medieval reckoning. That is why, in their churches, the medievalists did more than picture the apostles and the great heroes of the faith. They also carved into their church walls sculptural reliefs representing the activities of the doctor, lawyer, butcher, and baker. Everyone was significant in the total scheme of things, not just those who were called to formal ministry in the church. The medievalists recognized that everyone stood to gain or lose an incomprehensible treasure on the Day of Judgment toward which everything inevitably moves. They took God seriously. When we compare our church buildings to their church buildings it is obvious which age better understood the grand sweep of God's will. The medievalists had their faults and errors as we have ours, but one of them was not a small view of God.

Driven by one of the highest levels of creativity the world has ever known, medieval leaders were passionately involved in the shaping of their civilization. That required leaders in theology, business, architecture, music, education, art, economics, and politics; all of it important. It required a worldview capable of embracing the grand scheme and purpose of creation. Those leaders saw the big picture and spoke authoritatively about the kingdom of God and everyone's place in it. They communicated with such craft and passion that their monuments have stood as powerful witnesses through the centuries to this very day.

It is curious that today people use the term *medieval* to denote narrow-minded or unimaginative thinking, when the evidence demonstrates the opposite. A comparison of their creative efforts to ours can only end in the conclusion that their imaginations soared whereas ours flutter. A convocation of modern or post-modern architects could not design any kind of building that can approach the degree of architectural significance of even a minor medieval cathedral. Every cathedral or monastery was an opportunity for fresh ideas. Every one showed a progressive advance in knowledge, technology, and theology. In fact, when one of the two towers on the Cathedral of Notre-Dame at Chartres was destroyed by fire, they did not replace it with a duplicate. They built the most advanced design for the day. That is why the towers do not match today. Medieval leaders characteristically moved forward.

WHAT DOES THIS MEAN TO US?

Like the medieval leaders, we must look at change as creative opportunities built into the nature of things. We can be inspired by our knowledge of the past and of the existing universe to nurture creative changes in our families, schools, businesses, churches, and government. We can cooperate with the processes of God's kingdom, which are invisibly operating within all the activities on earth, including where you and I now work. This ongoing advance of the kingdom transforms the meaning of even the smallest task.

While that is happening, we know there will always be opposing forces, with leaders like those Churchill confronted, that are always focused upon outright destruction and evil. There are other leaders who appear to be less aggressive, but who bring mediocrity into whatever activity they engage. Then there is an additional and more common opposing force, ignorance—ignorance about the nature of leadership and how it is achieved. Destruction, evil, mediocrity, and ignorance are a formidable quartet we can oppose by enabling those who are leaders to be more effective in understanding and applying their leadership strengths. We need an increasing number of leaders who are persistent agents of constructive change and development, and we need these leaders in every activity that is necessary to community and civilization.

Note

1. Extract from a speech delivered by Sir Winston Churchill, May 13, 1940.

CHAPTER 2

THE GREAT CONTRADICTION

Leaders are people, and people live in a dual world. On one hand we are capable of extraordinary feats of daring and mettle. On the other, we know the shame of cowardice and weakness. We make things of beauty and, at times, even of splendor, but we also surround ourselves with ill-conceived environments, ugly merchandise, valueless entertainment, and shoddy services. It is obvious that a profound contradiction in our nature permeates not only our morals, but every activity with which we are involved, from the imaginative to the practical. As a result, the best that can be said about man remains true even alongside the worst. The gruesome ovens of Auschwitz are witnesses to the character of our species just as surely as the wonders of the Parthenon and Chartres Cathedral. As we deal with the nature of leadership, we must do so with the sobering awareness that neither the ovens nor the cathedrals could come into existence without the initiating activities of leaders. Leaders were involved with every phase of all those building projects, both repulsive and sublime. Leadership has been a part of every project that has cursed or blessed mankind since Eden.

LOOK AT THE EVIDENCE

Every cause, every crusade, every business, every organization, every product has been brought into being by a leader and can only be sustained by leaders. If the leaders are competent and appropriate for the situation, great benefits emerge, whether the leaders operate in multinational corporations or in schools. Such leaders know their mission and compel their organizations to focus upon the needs of the client. They follow up on what they promise to do. They train their people to be competent in service and back them up with effective systems and management. It is a pleasure to be the focus of their attention. That pleasure accompanies shopping at certain stores, working in certain corporations, going to certain schools, and attending certain churches. All of it is due to leaders who are positioned to make the right difference.

Of course, the reverse is true. If the leaders are incompetent or don't fit, a wretched harvest is inevitable. Most of us know corporations seemingly devoted to irritating everyone in their employ, classes our children hated to attend, inadequate athletic coaches, restaurants to which we made a once and final visit, committees that have driven us to despair, churches more interested in entertainment than in worship, and political campaigns that were doomed from the opening shot, all of it due to inadequate leaders.

The effect of a single leader, to say nothing of a hierarchy of them, can be enormous. The repercussions of their activities are vast. They make an impact not only upon production, but also upon the well-being and morale of thousands of people and their families, including you and me. Consumers, clients, workers, staff, professionals, volunteers, technicians, and children are continuously affected, for good or ill, by the work of leaders, on all levels. The successes and failures of our own immediate families, our businesses, churches, and schools, the national economy, and government itself are directly attributable to the quality of the people who lead them. They either advance us to success or bring about mediocrity. That is the sobering contradiction that has characterized the human race ever since Adam and Eve led the human race into the Fall. Since then we have been cursed with confusion, the evidence of which has been all too clear in every person and every organization since.

LOSING EDEN

By its nature the evidence of Eden is something that one cannot find. By its nature the evidence of sin is something that one cannot help finding.

G. K. Chesterton

As moderns, we sometimes do not connect the theology of the Fall to the reality of our daily lives. Although we know things are not the way they should be, we fail to adequately appreciate why that is. As a result we are confused about work and about leaders and leadership.

The loss of Eden was the loss of that for which we were made. Our hearts and lives were made for pleasure; the pleasure of craftsmanship in work and service to one another, the joy of right loves and friendships, and the rapture of knowing the One who created us. We lost it all. We forfeited our delights and have lived in bewilderment ever since. We are confused about why God made us and what we are to do in life. Too often, we don't know the work that fits us, who should lead us, or what goals are important. The kiss of death is upon all our efforts, so nothing seems to last. With uncomfortable frequency, we live in a limbo of the commonplace, with its aversion to distinctive work and energetic leadership.

Not only has sin corrupted individual lives with greed and pride, it has also opened the way to bureaucracy and incompetence in our organizations. It has distorted our ability to think clearly about how to manage joint efforts in those organizations and how to select and place people effectively.

Any ideas about leadership we have in our heads that are wrong will have unhappy results for us personally. But if we are leaders, those errors will inevitably have profound consequences for those we lead and, in turn, for those they lead. We can never know how far this influence may extend, but we can be sure that it goes far beyond what we suspect. One supervisor of twenty-five workers can affect one thousand hours of work in one week for good or ill. With that fact in mind we cannot even begin to assess what that can mean for those people and for the organization in an entire year. Wrong ideas about leadership lead to wrong practices that can be disastrous for a company or a community.

WHERE IS REALITY?

In response to all of this, there are those who may say, "Aren't you overreacting? Perhaps what we are dealing with are some mistakes in our methods of selecting and training leaders. But in this day of progress and technical know-how, what ideas could we now have about leadership that are not reliable? Isn't all this really a matter of improving what we already do?"

Generally, people tend to believe that our universities surely must know all there is to know about the nature of leadership, and so whatever tools they provide must be effective. That is not reality. Whatever is being done in our organizations in terms of defining, assessing, selecting, and training leaders is not working very well. It is not working well in the universities. It is not working well in the business schools, nor in the seminaries. It is not working well in churches, schools, or in government.

- How can it be working when almost all colleges and universities claim great skills in developing leaders, yet the majority of students in those same schools are in majors unrelated to their abilities and the careers they will eventually have?[1]

- How can it be working when a major corporate consultant we know of claims that only one in five executives with whom he has worked is actually gifted to be an executive?

- How can it be working when studies indicate that perhaps as many as a third of all companies that embark on Total Quality programs do not achieve their programmatic goals?[2]

- How can it be working when studies of job satisfaction reveal that the majority of people are in jobs that are not satisfying?[3]

- How can it be working when our nurturing institutions—the schools, churches, and families—have adapted models of leadership that are ineffective?

A VIVID EXAMPLE

For us, all of this came to a somewhat shocking focus when working with a department of thirteen employees of a Fortune 500 company not long ago. This was a company of considerable prestige, which is to say that they were doing a lot of things right. Our mandate was to build the group of thirteen into an effective team. On the way to that goal, we were inspired to ask three questions of that group.

Question 1. *"How many years of work for this company are represented here?"* Given the variety in their ages, there were an equal variety of answers. When we added them up, they totaled to more than a century of productivity on the part of the group. Specifically, it added up to 113 years. That is a hefty amount of time, consuming much energy and many resources.

Question 2. *"How many bosses, managers, leaders, and supervisors did you have during all those years?"* It added up to a total of eighty-six leaders.

Question 3. *"How many of those bosses, managers, leaders, and supervisors were on your side? In other words, you knew they were working hard to make sure you and those with whom you were working were successful. They were for you."* The answer was thirteen.

Not even a third of the leaders were being effective as leaders. Seventy-three out of eighty-six had the authority of leadership but apparently were without the gifts of leadership or were gifted but without effective training for leadership.

We knew we had discovered valid data because we had questioned the people who knew best. We had asked the followers. They knew who the real leaders were. They certainly knew whether or not they were being supported in their efforts. So even if we were extraordinarily generous in providing a margin for error, we still ended up with miserable conclusions.

UNHAPPY SURPRISE

Of course, we wouldn't have asked the those questions if we hadn't expected a somewhat low number, but we were as surprised as the thirteen participants at how low it actually was. We can assure you that we were not dealing with a company unconcerned about productivity or a company unsophisticated in matters of management. Yet we were looking at a company, like most others, where the assumptions being made about management and leadership were so distorted that out of eighty-six who were appointed to be leaders, only thirteen made a positive difference to the people who were reporting to them. Can you imagine the kind of waste that represents when multiplied by 113 individual years of effort? It boggles the mind.

What do those numbers mean to job satisfaction and to morale? How do the victims of mediocre leadership influence the attitudes developed by their children as to the value and meaning of work? What about energy levels, morale, and their effect on other employees? What about productivity? What about the diminished growth and its effect on the nation's economy? Chain reaction thinking must be applied to the issue of leadership if we are to understand its power. Everything and everybody is affected.

THE GOOD NEWS

The story of the Fall that we mentioned is, of course, not the whole story. Ultimately the good news of redemption follows. Breaking through our confusion is the rousing voice of Jesus Christ, whose words sweeps aside any pessimism.

> I am come that they might have life, and that they might have it
> more abundantly. *(John 10:10 KJV)*

Where there is death, Jesus brings life. Where there is error, He brings understanding. Where there is confusion, He brings clarity. Where there is mediocrity, He brings creativity. He brought to His followers then and brings to His followers now the ability to reverse the stultified thinking that cripples people and their organizations. He brings fresh understanding and effective ways of acting. What's more, He brings the power for change wherever He finds a leader willing to make a difference. That has been exemplified in the person of the apostle Peter. The intimidated Peter, who betrayed his Lord in the story of the crucifixion, became a founding leader of the church. There was a remarkable transformation of his life that brought him from an abyss of despair to key leadership in the most influential organization the earth has ever seen.

God can reverse even the most impossible situations. It is with that optimism we hope to stimulate fresh thinking about the meaning and the work of leadership. To do this, we first must focus upon two mistakes prevalent in our thinking about leaders and leadership. Once we get rid of ideas that do not work, we can better engage concepts that do. That includes equipping you to discover and understand your leadership gifts, find your rightful place, and engage in those exploits for which you were born.

The two mistakes we will address are these:

1. Assuming that we can make leaders.
2. Assuming that leaders are paragons.

Notes

1. The College Placement Council and the National Institute of Education sponsored the research by Bisconte and Solomon, *College Education on the Job,* 1961. For example, 38 percent ended up in business career roles from administration to accounting, although less than one in five majored in business.

2. A Study by Arthur Anderson & Co. indicates that a third of the companies who have embarked on some kind of Total Quality program or Total Quality Management achieve what they intended by engaging in those programs. Our direct observation of TQ has been in the corporate scene, where it is clear that there has been little observation of how people fit into such programs beyond the expectation that they buy off on TQ principles before engaging the process. Smaller organizations may have done better on that score.

3. Marketing Survey and Research Corporation, Princeton, N.J., reported in 1976 that a sixteen-year study involving 350,000 persons and 1,000 corporations concluded that four out of five people experience a job misfit. Yankelovich, Shelley, and White, Inc., a public opinion firm, reported in 1987 that only 13 percent of all Americans found their work truly meaningful.

MISTAKE #1

Assuming that We Make Leaders

Before I formed you in the womb I knew you,
before you were born I set you apart.
JEREMIAH 1:5 NIV

CHAPTER 3

WHERE DO WE
GET LEADERS?

F rom where do leaders come? Do you have to go to college or to
graduate school to become a leader? Can you become a leader by
taking the right courses?

If we are to believe the brochures of colleges and universities, both
secular and denominational, from coast to coast, we must conclude that
they produce the leaders. The language used by some colleges appears
almost to guarantee the acquisition of leadership abilities if you attend
their school. Visits to their campuses usually involve introductions to
bright students who clearly exemplify outstanding leadership. But the
question is not whether there are leaders in our nation's schools. We all
know that there are many outstanding leaders on every campus. The
question is whether they are leaders because of the educational methods
of the schools. What courses create these leaders? What is the leadership-
formation technology?

One college, for example, in describing the objectives of its School
of Business Administration, affirms that the role of leadership is critical in
the modern business system. Yet, in its course listings, not one course

appears to be aimed at the development of leadership. There are courses that present models and theories of management and organizational behavior, but none in actual leadership development. Leaders are expected to somehow emerge out of the informal and formal processes of college life. There is no expectation that leadership should be addressed in any comprehensive way.

We do know that leadership appears on college campuses in all kinds of settings, from athletic to academic. We believe that to be true because the leaders arrived as leaders and responded to the opportunities the schools provided for leadership. Those opportunities for the expression and sharpening of leadership skills are important features of quality education. They should be valued, but without assuming that somehow they can *impart* leadership abilities. We also need to make room in our thinking for those we know are prominent leaders, but whose leadership abilities were not recognized until after their school years. Then there are leaders everywhere who never went to college and who made their own opportunities.

CAN A SCHOOL MAKE YOU A LEADER?

This matter of what schools can or cannot do is important to understand. Before we consider whether we can become leaders by taking the right courses, let us first look at what schools do with the simple matter of careers, not even including the matter of leadership within those careers.

It is assumed that law schools make lawyers, medical schools make doctors, seminaries make preachers, and colleges make teachers. That assumption is so powerfully imbedded into our culture, it is rarely questioned. We have worked with thousands of professionals over the years, and it has amazed us to hear the reasons people give for having decided to take on the careers in which they ended up. Too often, the reasons have more to do with outside influences than with a passion for the vocation they have chosen. How, we wonder, can adults assume that being trained in a profession will stimulate a love for that profession, much less the genius for it?

Can schools create professionals? A simple survey will provide a swift answer. Let us look at a profession with which we are all familiar: education. How many teachers really turned on the lights for you in any school you attended? Stretching from first grade to the highest level you attained, how many teachers made a substantial difference to you?

If you are like many of us, you will conclude not many. But the ones we do remember, we remember with great fondness and appreciation.

They made a large and sometimes colossal impact upon our lives. We may even remember their names, no matter how many years have passed since we sat in their classes. They were gifted teachers and, whatever level from grade school to graduate school, they made us learn. They did this sometimes in spite of us, and even in spite of our aversion to the subjects they taught. They were the teachers who made the classroom come alive. We are profoundly indebted to them.

But we also know those infamous teachers for whom thirty years of teaching practice failed to dim a stupefying ability to bring all students, strong and weak, to the acme of boredom. They were backed by allies stretching through our past, teacher after teacher, who may not have achieved such pinnacles of tedium, but faithful, credentialed, even likable, paid professionals who could not bring us to the excitement of learning. Teacher certification assures us that they were teachers by profession. We, the clients, know they were not teachers by gift.

Apparently the places from which they graduated failed to turn them into the teachers they claimed to produce. Yet those very same colleges also graduated brilliant teachers. The variable here is not the institution, nor the factor of intelligence. It is the inherent gifts that the student-teachers bring to the professional training. Even the acquisition of advanced degrees does not improve poor teaching. Thousands upon thousands of students can witness to that reality. Teaching is a gift that is honed by education and experience but not acquired by either. What is true about teachers is true about all the professions. No amount of training will make a nonmanager a manager, a nonpoet a poet, or a nonleader a leader. Ask the employees, the readers, and the followers.

Place a nonmanager into management training and out will come a nonmanager who knows about management and might even teach the next course. But observe the trained nonmanager in a management situation, and it will be clear that though he or she may occupy the position of manager, little actual management is taking place.

THE DIFFERENCE BETWEEN GIFTS AND SKILLS

Much of the confusion in dealing with these issues is the failure to differentiate between skills and gifts. Skills can be acquired. We can learn how to speak French, Welsh, or Norwegian. We can learn to use the computer, even if we would prefer not to. We can learn how to play any number of sports. There are courses of all kinds, from academic subjects to house building, available one way or another in most communities. We can enroll in them and, for whatever reason, acquire skills—some practical, some otherwise.

But there is another class of skills. They are the ones that draw us, by the tens of thousands, to stadiums, concert halls, civic centers, museums, theaters, and galleries all over the country. There we see abilities demonstrated on such a high level of virtuosity that we know what we are witnessing is more than the demonstration of mere skills. Some high level of competence is operating behind the skills we see, whether athletic or artistic. We are encountering nothing less than gifts, the gifts that drive the skills. The outcome is a level of performance that cannot be attained merely by practice or training by an outstanding coach. That level of genius is driven by gifts that are inherently part of who the performers are as persons. This can be illustrated by a simple formula.

$$GIFTS + SKILLS = TALENT$$

With that in mind, we can see that though any number of us may take piano lessons with good results, very, very few could ever consider a career as a concert pianist. Vladimir Horowitz and Rudolf Serkin did not build their formidable careers on mere skills. Such levels of musicianship can only be achieved through a masterful grasp of what a performance must be and an expressive ability to deliver it. Those abilities are God-given gifts and cannot be attained by any amount of practice, though incessant practice is required to bring them into fruition.

A linguist is more than a person who has taken lessons in Italian. People can learn how to write, sketch, or do their taxes. But it takes more than that to be a novelist, artist, or an accountant.

FOUR KINDS OF CAPABILITIES

We can clear up a lot of confusion for ourselves when we become a bit more precise in analyzing the abilities people display in their jobs and leisure activities. Here are four categories that may be useful.

1. **Practical skills**, such as cooking, repairing, and typing
2. **Leisure skills**, such as golf, weaving, and fly-fishing
3. **Gifted skills**, those abilities that are used to express a gift
4. **Gifts**, such as teaching, sculpting, managing, and acting

Given these categories, we can see that it is possible for someone to learn the skills involved in presenting academic material to students. Indeed, there are situations where teachers need not be able to do much more than that. But none of this should be confused with possessing authentic teaching gifts. Similarly, it is possible for someone to learn some skills of leadership. The corporal who has been told by the sergeant to take over the drill team might exercise skills adequate to the situation, but surely we want more if he is going to lead us out of a foxhole to take enemy-held territory.

DOES THAT EXCLUDE YOU?

Contrasting leadership skills against leadership gifts may create a problem. It does not permit the person who is not a leader the opportunity to become a leader by acquiring the necessary skills. In fact, it may appear to leave you out. However, what the world has missed is the wonderful variety of leaders. For example, when God made trees, He did not make one authorized version. Variety upon variety, species upon species cover the entire globe, everything from the hard-edged Joshua tree to the multi-trunked Banyan. Similarly, the variety of leaders is astounding. We tend to miss it because the glasses provided by our contemporary society, through which the subject is viewed, afford much too narrow a picture. You will discover a far more effective a way to understand and use your leadership abilities if you do not allow anyone to press you into a mold that does not fit you, but instead discover your own leadership style and the arena in which it can best operate.

We also recognize that a number of readers may have an interest in the subject of leadership, but not because they want to become leaders. It would be ludicrous to even slightly suggest that therefore they are persons of lesser importance. Their disinterest in being leaders is because it has nothing to do with who they are. That is not how God made them. Obviously, from the Designer's point of view, the value of anyone has to do with being an authentic person, not with being a leader. Attempting to pursue the goals of a leader without the gifts of a leader is nothing but an empty exercise. It offers as much satisfaction as that enjoyed by a lion attempting to sing like a lark.

CHAPTER 4

THE GREAT
CRAMMING
PROCESS

A fragment from the book of Proverbs expresses the theme of this chapter.

> For as he thinketh in his heart, so is he. *(Proverbs 23:7 KJV)*

The context in which this verse appears warns us to be selective about the people with whom we associate. The phrase is striking for its simplicity in connecting the content of what we dwell on with who we reveal ourselves to be. That connection is especially fascinating as we consider what we feed upon intellectually. There is a real danger in not being judicious about the theories or concepts we embrace. That is especially true for those who do not tend to develop a worldview thoroughly informed by biblical perspectives.

WHO INFLUENCES US THE MOST?

We should ask this question when we think about leaders. From where do our basic ideas about the nature of leadership come?

Whether or not you work for one, the corporation probably affects the way you think about leaders more than your church does. That might seem farfetched. After all, the Bible has a lot to say about leaders, all of it more profound than anything to be discovered in corporate training. However, we have found in the church and in church-related institutions that a theology of leadership is one thing, practice another. Practice is usually modeled after the corporate world. Years of working with both corporate and church leaders have convinced us that corporate culture is the most influential force in defining leadership for all our institutions.

The influence of corporations upon our assumptions about leaders is not because they are necessarily creative. It is because corporations are everywhere and affect many people. They also have a profit margin to produce, so they tend to be aggressive about the selection and development of leaders who bring that about. Given this drive, they keep re-addressing the process of leadership and management development. We see this not only in training and consulting activities, but also in magazine and book publishing. The number of books aimed at corporate executives, or that have been written by corporate consultants, is a sizable industry in itself.

Given the wealth of material, one might assume that in the corporate world the science or the art of leadership must be pretty well nailed down by now. However, as with the universities, that is not what has happened. There is no common foundation upon which ideas about leadership are developed. Most of the ideas about leadership emerge out of the ongoing intercourse between business and universities. Each is a resource for the other. As a result, most of the books on leadership tend to do the same thing. They all prescribe some kind of model leader or model manager for everyone to emulate.

The leadership models are everywhere in our society; in companies of all sizes, in schools of all kinds, and in churches of all denominations. The assumption is that to become an effective leader you must duplicate the model. Leadership training and development, from churches to corporations, are almost totally based on models. That means that if you are a leader or expect to be one, or work with one, you are forced along one path in your thinking; one path without suspecting there might be alternatives. We can summarize that path as follows.

1. Find a model for a leader.
2. Train everyone to imitate it.

MODELS AND MODES

A survey of leadership and management books reveals not only that they are all committed to portraying a model, but that the model keeps changing from book to book. Most of the books were written in reaction to whatever was current leadership or management practice at the time the book was written. Here are a few:

> The Functional Leader
> Management by Intimidation
> The Great Man Theory
> Functional Leadership
> Management by Objectives
> Reality Centered Leadership
> The Charismatic Leader
> Group Centered Leadership
> The Relational Leader
> Management by Walking Around
> Entrepreneurial Leadership

What we conclude is that these models are a matter of fashion. They come and they go, with a few of them having had major influence. For example, Management by Objectives (MBO) recognized the requirement for an organization to set goals and assess its progress in achieving them. That makes sense. But the idea was systematized for *every* employee. The tremendous faith in the model skirted a simple fact: *What motivates those who develop the overall direction of the organization does not necessarily motivate all the individuals in the organization.* Many people simply do not operate in terms of goals. They think it is right and proper for the company to worry about goals while they worry about the work at hand. So for an organization to expend resources in order to get all employees to articulate their goals can be more bureaucratic than motivational for most people.

SHOULD EVERYONE SET GOALS?

Some readers who are motivated by goals will probably react negatively to that question. They naturally believe goals are a necessity since they are motivated by them and probably would flourish in an MBO system. Those who are not motivated by goals, but who operate in some other fashion, will probably agree with what has been stated. However, they may feel a bit guilty about it, since the dominant models in our culture do feature goals. There are goal-setting seminars everywhere; in business, in churches, and in schools. Goals are more than an objective in our culture. They have become a value. If you set goals, you are good. If you are disinterested in setting goals, you are not so good. Trainers always seem interested in transmogrifying non–goal setters into goal setters. Is it possible that there are people who live effectively without being driven by goals? The answer, simply, is yes. Some of them are our most creative citizens. They know their goals at the point they achieve them.

WE ALL KNOW THE RIGHT WAY

We all tend to devise models that are workable for ourselves and people like us. We are dumbfounded when they do not work for others. But when we do that, we are simply universalizing what works for us, not thinking through what works best for others. That makes just as much sense as applying New York City traffic rules to hikers in the Amazon. Each of us looks through the lens of what interests us. If we are highly relational, we react to the relational problems that exist in organizations and accordingly devise a corrective model. If we are authoritarian, we are preoccupied with hierarchical structures and with who has the power to do what. If we have a charismatic personality, we value opportunities to present ideas that make an impact upon the masses. The person, or persons, who originated the MBO model probably wrote out goals for his private life before he told us how to get serious about objectives for business. We all tend to make norms and principles out of our particular way of operating.

NO NORM?

We are not suggesting that there are no valid principles and that everything is relative. Nor do we believe that models are useless. What we are saying is that problems naturally arise when we develop models before considering if they are appropriate for the situation. When a machinist makes a prototype gear for a new machine, we all know he has taken on an appropriate task. Every gear manufactured for the new machine must be an exact duplicate of a prototype. Machines will not work without that kind of precise imitation.

Similarly, we can rightly expect all leaders to be honest and just. That is a model of character that can be justifiably universalized because it is appropriate for all leaders in all situations. A person who cheats, is dishonest, unfair, and a liar should not be a leader; not in business, not in schools, not in church nor in government. Even the leaders who do lie, for example, do not want others to lie to them. So, they, too, give allegiance to the model. This model of behavior makes sense anywhere and for any time. It was valid in the year 1 and in the year 1734 and in any other year, including the one we are in.

But a model for character is one thing. How a person should operate, in particular, as a leader is a different matter. Precise models that work so well in engineering do not work very well with people. And that is the difficulty we find in today's culture. A way of thinking that works well in technology gets applied to people, where it does not work. We cannot measure personalities in the same way we can record the dimensions of a piston. We cannot design the development of a leader in the same way we could designate the steps in the manufacture of an automobile. We cannot design a human prototype and from it develop as many leaders as we want. That's not the way it works.

WHERE DO WE BEGIN?

Before we develop any theory or a model about people, let us do something novel. Let's begin with people instead of a theory. Let's take a commonsense look at how real people actually operate. Then let us build our understanding of them, us, and subsequently of leadership on the basis of how people behave in real life. The next chapter will discuss four principles we have found to be basic to an understanding of how people operate, principles we expect you, too, have experienced in one way or another.

CHAPTER 5

———⌒⌒⌒———

LOOKING
AT PEOPLE

WHEN PEOPLE ARE THEMSELVES

Our first example comes from many years ago as a youngster growing up in New York City, where we learned how to play stickball. Using a soft rubber ball and a cut-off broomstick, we modified baseball so that we could play the game in the midst of traffic and parked cars.

Like baseball or softball played in any town, anywhere, stickball required choosing teams. It also involved filling each position with the best talent. All of this, of course, required considerable heated negotiation. On our street we usually would argue over Bobby. Both teams wanted him, seemingly at the price of blood or a black eye, because he was the best hitter. Noisy argument preceded the selection of every position. Your status in the neighborhood was indicated by the decibel level your name inspired.

How did we know who should play what position? By seeing each player in action many times. We exploited our knowledge of consistent past behavior as the basis for our decisions. That makes common sense for selecting kids for a team, and that is the approach we recommend for selecting adults for positions in organizations. If we, as adults, could be as wise about selecting people as we were as children, we could radically improve the effectiveness of most of our organizations. Repeated cracks of a bat against a baseball is wonderfully useful evidence. What is true about success in stickball, baseball, and softball is true about success in any job.

ENCOUNTERS WITH COMPUTERS

Our second example focuses on learning in the context of an office. In this example, more people have had to learn how to use computers than have been interested in using them. As these people went about familiarizing themselves with the computers, it was evident that they had different attitudes and different ways of going about learning how to operate the new equipment.

Anne, Brian, Terry, Ruth, and Erik

All computers arrive with manuals, a couple for actually operating the computer and others for understanding the software programs in it. When Anne was required to learn how to operate the computer, she read the manuals from cover to cover before she would even consider turning on the machine. In fact, she read the material twice before touching the *on* button. Then there was Brian, who confesses that he used the manuals as a doorstop while he surreptitiously turned the computer on to see how it worked. He played and experimented his way to competence without ever reading the manuals, except for occasional reference when he had a problem.

Terry was torn between her dislike for reading the manuals and wanting to use the equipment correctly. She simply does not experiment, so she bought videos that demonstrated everything. Ruth would have nothing to do with the manuals, videos, or experimenting. She walked out of her office and asked everyone within hearing, "Does anyone here know how to work this computer?"

Meanwhile, her friend Erik shook his head in disbelief at her casual approach as he left for a training class that promised to bring him up to speed quickly. His assessment? Training with an expert is the only way to learn.

What can we conclude from this? Each person learns in his or her own way.

Why Learn the Computer?

If you ask individuals why they learned how to use the computer you will not be given uniform answers. Some were attracted to the machine even though they had no professional justification for owning one, whereas others had to be coerced. Look at the way our quintet responded to the question.

ANNE: "Because my boss wanted me to." Anne seems to be motivated to respond to requirements.

BRIAN: "It's an interesting tool to use." It may be that the opportunity to discover new things got him interested.

TERRY: "It was necessary for me to do my job well." Convince her that she would be more effective in her work and she will be interested.

RUTH: "All my friends are using them now." Ruth tends to be attracted to that which her peers already have become involved.

ERIK: "People need to upgrade their skills." He is always interested in any learning that can be considered professional growth.

What can we conclude from this? *Each person is triggered into action for different reasons.*

WHY PLAY FOOTBALL?

Our third example of how people actually operate is from athletics. In this field people have always operated with a high regard for models. As the manager of a well-known baseball team put it, "I treat all my players the same." That would be fine if he were in court, but on the field he would do a better job if he recognized each player's uniqueness. In contrast, we talked to a pitching coach for another team who described for us how he had been working through each player's natural style. He found that gets best results.

God made each athlete unique, no matter what a coach may think. That was dramatized for me by a Denver Broncos team member who decided to retire from professional football. He believed he was at an age where it made sense to consider another career while he was still an outstanding player and his reputation was intact. As a spiritual man, he sought God's direction while considering possibilities. As an individual who recognized the value of using others' skills, he asked if we would assist him in discovering what gifts he was using in football could be transferred to another vocation.

The first step we took was to prepare a report providing a portrait of his gifts, usually detailed by fifty-five to sixty gift elements. As we explained how those gifts worked, he pointed out the absence of the word *competition* in the report. We responded, "Although you are in a competitive profession, that isn't exactly what drives you to do so well." He thought that was an unusual idea and said so. "All professional football players are competitive!" Our response was to say that although competition is required for a game to take place, that is not necessarily what directly motivates every player. We then pointed out to him various players on his team as examples.

- **The Calculator**: He always keeps his eye on the ball, his coach, and the coach of the opposing team. If we could get into his mind we would see that he picks up clues like a detective and swiftly schemes out what he will do in response. That is where his game is. The more complex the game, the more fun, sometimes even when his team loses.
- **The Star**: He is always responding to the fans, waving, working the crowd, and always making himself available for autographs. He says, "Winning without a big crowd to cheer you is not much fun."
- **The Scorer**: For him, winning is meaningless unless his personal statistics are good. He can give you the numbers for every game he has played and can tell you who comes close to, or beats, his averages.
- **The Overcomer**: He ignores the statistics but is triggered by the impossible challenge, at which point he almost always comes through. His coach does not understand his "uneven performance."
- **The Strategist**: He loves football because he loves executing strategies. While his buddy strains to understand a play, he visually swallows football diagrams whole.
- **The Competitor**: For him, competition is not merely an ingredient but is the most meaningful factor in playing football. But even here, competitors are not all the same. Whereas one competes head-to-head ("I got him"), others think in terms of the team ("We got them").

What can we conclude from this? Each person is motivated to bring about particular results.

MISFIT SITUATIONS PROVIDE EVIDENCE

Our fourth example comes from observing people in jobs that do not fit. We know a man who has an excellent reputation for precision machining, but he is bored by his well-paying job. What he loves is volunteer work in a downtown soup kitchen, where he can do a variety of tasks that end with directly helping people. He has always loved helping people.

There is the sales manager who wishes she were out selling, instead of sitting at a desk. Her company assumes she will enable the salespeople to do what she used to do so well before she became a manager. But she doesn't want to work with salespeople who won't buy. She wants to work with potential clients who will.

Additional examples are all about us. There is the mom who is bored with working at a prestigious law firm and really prefers to be a homemaker, because in that capacity she can do a variety of tasks exactly the way she would prefer. Then there is the engineer who wants to develop new products but is instead required to solve problems and fix what is broken. We also know a teacher who enjoys helping the underdog succeed but who has been "rewarded" with a class of gifted students.

What can we conclude from these misfit situations? *People are motivated to do only certain kinds of things aside from whether or not their jobs call for those efforts.*

People will seek ways outside their jobs to do activities that interest them if their jobs offer no opportunities to put those interests into play. That explains hobbies. The reason hobbies developed was so people could use gifts and skills not called for in their jobs.

THE ASSUMPTION THAT FAILED

The world assumes that people are like clay to be molded into whatever society needs them to be or whatever their families encourage them to be. The evidence all about us does not support that assumption. There are formerly poor, undereducated, inner-city kids who, as adults, have achieved feats of leadership their families could not even imagine. The specific gifts necessary to attain their outstanding achievements were not acquired in school or on the streets. They already had them.

COMMON SENSE

People are gifted. That is their nature. If we look at what they are gifted to do, we can draw conclusions about what they would be good at vocationally. That is common sense. We cannot be sure a person is a problem solver because of any kind of certification. We know problem solvers because we have observed them bringing about abundant solutions. We know who can solve people problems because we have observed them repeatedly and successfully take care of problems involving relationships. We know who the technical problem solvers are because we have observed them consistently solve problems involving technology.

Making crystal clear to candidates what kind of person you want for the job does not assure that is what you will get. Agreement with a job description is not going to transform anyone into what is needed. Nor will repeated reviews of a job description motivate an employee to do what is required. People cannot be molded or remolded at the whim of managers, bosses, personnel departments, trainers, or hiring managers. What most people will do is to reshape the job so they can do what they are motivated to do, if they can get away with it. If it is the boss who is doing the reshaping, he or she does get away with it, whether or not it is ultimately best for the organization.

BEING PROFESSIONAL

None of this should be construed as an argument against certification or education or degrees or licenses. Training and professional standards are important to craftsmanship in any field. For example, electricity is too powerful to be harnessed by unqualified people, so it is necessary to train and credential electricians and electrical engineers to handle it. However, there is a big difference between electricians or electrical engineers who are innovative and those who are good at maintaining an operation. Credentials don't tell that story. There is a difference between those who are motivated to repair an electrical supply system and those who are gifted at designing one. Credentials don't describe that reality, either. Credentials are important, but they have serious limitations. They assure a certain level of technical know-how, but they cannot describe the situations to which that expertise should be applied.

When we define people only in terms of training or education or degrees, we get an all too limited picture of what they bring to their work. Somewhere in an organization at this moment, failure is imminent, yet there exists also someone who has the knowledge and the ability to reverse that failure. Somewhere there is a stagnant organization, but there are also mavericks working within that organization who could be empowered to create change. Somewhere resources are waning, but at that "somewhere" there is also someone who knows how and where to acquire more of whatever is needed.

For any given task, there are people gifted to take it on. Where profits are falling or growth is stymied, there are those who, if brought in, could find out why. There are others who can develop effective strategies in view of that data. Where people are fearful, there are those who can give hope. Where technical breakthroughs are needed, there are innovators who can deliver the goods. These people are all leaders—leaders of different kinds, with different gifts operating on different levels. But one thing they have in common: their God-given gifts bring about specific results that fit, not anywhere, but in particular situations.

THE REALITY OF PEOPLE AND THEIR GIFTS

What a delightful picture we have when we look beyond the idea of people as a mass of mere potential, when we realize that each person is already motivated to bring about quality results somewhere. People are not blobs of clay to be shaped by our needs. They are gifted persons already designed in marvelous detail. If we enable them and equip them and train them according to who they are already designed to be, we will get excellence and competence.

This is not some feel-good Pollyanna idea. It is a description of the nature of humanity. The reason civilization has gotten so far, in spite of the curse of the Fall, is because of the gifts of individuals being focused upon appropriate activities. The reason we are not further along than we are has much to do with people being misused and misusing themselves by taking on that which has little to do with their gifts. We may do that innocently by adapting errant goals provided by our culture. We may do that out of greed, attempting to satisfy goals we have no business looking at. Either way, we end up with career misfit, leadership bankruptcy, and confusion.

We have found four facts to be basic to the nature of human achievement as observed in the examples given above and as documented by thousands of cases in our files. The degree to which our policies, procedures, and systems involving people are informed by these facts is the degree to which we will encourage excellence.

1. *Each person is unique.* By definition, that means being the only one, like no other. This is a charmingly simple fact, but it has massive implications. It means we cannot lead everyone in the

same way nor educate, manage, and nurture everyone in a standardized manner and expect excellence.

2. *Each person is individually gifted.* By definition that means having gifts distinguished from those of everyone else—being endowed with a notable capacity, a knack for achieving something particular. There may be similarities in types of gifts, but each person operates in a particular way. There are, for example, many kinds of managers, organizers, communicators, and developers, each applying his or her gifts to different areas of interest to achieve differing results. The benefit of knowing this is that it gives us a foundation to build on in terms of job-fit. It gives us a way to understand which roles fit an individual and which do not. Knowledge of our gifts equips us to fend off those who would approach us as if we were raw material for their projects.

3. *Gifted capacities are complex.* They can be described, but they cannot be measured. They are dynamic, with each element impacting upon another in a complexity of motivated intensity. Knowing this enables us to avoid simplistic labels. It is the door to exquisite precision in developing and managing people.

4. *Every person is motivated.* By definition that means possessing initiative and drive to accomplish something in particular and not necessarily what one's friends, family, supervisors, or teachers want. The secret of effective management is to engage people in doing what they are gifted to do, which is to say what they are motivated to do. That saves us from the constant monitoring required to get people to do what they actually have no interest in doing. People who are paid to do what they are motivated to do are inoculated against burnout unless they have been unwise in balancing work with leisure.

These four facts add up to the conclusion that there is a powerful resource of energy in each person to accomplish particular results. When anyone or any organization happens to tap that energy, we see what God always intended. We observe people doing what they were made to do, love to do, are energized to do, and can repeatedly do and remain satisfied. Those who are gifted to design never get tired of coming up with new designs. Conceptualizers never tire of conceptualizing. Helpers don't usually tire of helping. Organizers repeatedly organize. Clearly, these facts do not support the idea that mankind makes its own leaders. God makes the leaders.

Professionally, having had the opportunity to view the gifts of thousands of people in detail, we can boldly state that no one duplicates anyone else. We still are amazed at the wonderful interior landscape that marks individuality. This is not only an aesthetic wonder; it is the most practical and powerful resource available in attaining quality results anywhere human effort is going to make a difference.

MISTAKE #2

Assuming that Leaders Are Paragons

So much perfection argues rottenness somewhere.
Beatrice Webb

CHAPTER 6

———⊙〜✐✐✐〜⊙———

ATTAINING
PERFECTION

T he first mistake, discussed in the last three chapters, involves the making of the leader. The second mistake, discussed here, involves the individual performance of the leader. The first affects how we define, develop, and select leaders. The second has an impact upon the individual leader's realization of success.

THE CRIPPLING IDEAL

Every career field tends to have a vision of what constitutes the ideal professional. Many people strive, or feel they should strive, to become whatever that ideal happens to be. The stories they tell about each other whenever they talk shop naturally reaffirm the kind of person they all see as the model for success in their business, trade, or profession. And so we end up with the Ideal Athlete, Ideal Executive, Ideal Pastor, Ideal Salesperson, Ideal Counselor, Ideal Carpenter, and Ideal Surgeon. Now this is not entirely bad, especially when the focus is upon whatever leads to craftsmanship in that profession. Seeking to stay on top of new developments and getting additional professional training, for example, is a matter of attaining excellence. That benefits everybody. But when the vision moves away from enhanced professional craftsmanship to focus upon a glorified personal image of the ideal professional, it becomes counterproductive. Energy is then spent attempting to become somebody other than who we actually are. In other words, what we are dealing with is a form of idolatry.

This vision of the professional paragon has, in fact, become a powerful myth we all tend to share as part of our culture. *The Fountainhead,* by Ayn Rand, has been around for half a century precisely because it celebrates this myth.[1] The hero is an architect who must, like many of us, work out of an office. But under the direction of the author, he is transfigured into Architect-as-Prophet. His individual success-in-spite-of-provincialism is magnified to Wagnerian proportions. This myth says life only has meaning for architects if they can reproduce such drama.

What kind of plot do we ordinary mortals engage in our imaginations? Well, we probably picture ourselves as climbing to ever-grander levels of leadership, with no doubt a very clear image in our minds of what we need to look like when we finally get to the top. We also know that presently we do not look like that. The point here is that we will never look like that, nor should we. Achieving higher and higher levels of professional leadership or management only fits certain people. We must jettison the idea that being president of an organization is in itself success. It can only be success for particular persons who have the appropriate gifts and the experience for that office. Being president is not an award; it is a function and requires particular gifts. The president is not the one who stands out from all the rest as the woman or man for all seasons, nor is he or she the one who has learned how to acquire more gifts than the others who competed for the position. But that is generally how a president is perceived, and such perceptions lead to confusion.

THE PARAGON LEADER

There is hardly a book or seminar on leadership in any setting that does not provide a list of the distinguishing features of leadership, the acquisition of which, we are assured, make up the outstanding leader.

> Leaders are visionaries.
> Leaders are independent thinkers.
> Leaders make swift decisions.
> Leaders always delegate.
> Leaders are entrepreneurial.

Leaders set clear goals.
Leaders inspire and motivate the troops.
Leaders are strategic thinkers.

The insistence that we think solely in terms of ideal characteristics leaves us little room to realistically develop and place leaders effectively in any organization. For example, let us look at an exception to the first item on the above list, "Leaders are visionaries."

Leaders are visionaries

Dave built a business around a technical invention developed by his partner, William. William has little business sense, but lots of technical ingenuity. Dave, a strong entrepreneur, has been able to develop financial resources to back the business, hire good managers, and get everyone enthused about the product and sales.

The only visionary aspects to this particular business are covered by a long-range business plan developed by consultants. Is Dave a leader? In view of what he has already accomplished we must conclude that he is, but he is no visionary. It was obvious to everyone that the invention William came up with filled a long-term technical need. Dave merely moved from that fact to a logical strategy for building a very successful business. He has never been grasped by a vision. He has made sensible moves in face of some obvious facts.

Now it may be that the company will eventually come to a point in its development where it will require visionary development, especially if new products or new markets become part of the plan. At that point, Dave will probably be faulted for not "growing with the business." A crisis will ensue in which probably no one will fully know what the problem actually is. Therefore, none of the solutions will be precise, and every one of them will be expensive, at least in terms of morale if not other business resources. It will begin with Dave's being advised that he needs to develop a vision. That, of course, will be another way of saying that he must become a different kind of leader. The very gifts that were appreciated for bringing the company into being now will be judged as no longer useful.

That is the kind of scenario that can emerge when we operate with models that are inadequate to the realities of an organization and of how people are designed. The solution in Dave's case would be to look for alternative resources. Those could be other executives or consultants who have the appropriate gifts to complement him. If this were a business that required a visionary leader on a permanent basis, then Dave would have to make way for such a person and move to a different function where he could use his gifts, perhaps in another company.

In a situation such as Dave's, failure to appreciate the precision with which people are designed will likely end in bad feelings, misunderstanding, political maneuvering, nervous clients, and low morale. That which was established with joy, energy, and optimism will end up like a soap opera. It would be possible to fill this book with stories of unnecessary organizational trauma because participants made decisions based on the false assumptions about people with which most of us have been reared.

WHY THE IDEAL PROTOTYPES?

Why all this effort to develop ideal leadership prototypes when we cannot find anywhere, anyone who has reached such a zenith of leadership excellence? Who are these people who have acquired all the gifts and all the desirable attributes by which we judge others? They don't exist. There is no one, nor can there be. Why? Simply because that is not how God made human beings. No one has all the gifts. Why then do we use such standards? We should not be preoccupied with models that have no pragmatic use and do not reflect the reality of what God has created.

MORE EVIDENCE

It would be one thing if this preoccupation with idealized prototypes appeared here and there as one theoretical option. But what we are dealing with is wholesale capitulation to ideas that have bred problems for every organization in our country. High levels of job-misfit and inadequate management are everywhere, not because there are so many inept workers, but because the workers are not in the appropriate places.

Consider one of the tools used to further this unhappy condition, personality tests. We are all familiar with them. People take them as part of hiring procedures and in therapeutic settings. They are such a part of our culture they even appear in popularized versions as a form of entertainment in magazines. Since they are tests, they require a standard against which the subject will be compared. The result is a score that indicates where the person is strong and where weak. After the results of the tests are analyzed, what usually happens is that the strengths are ignored for the most part. Much attention is then given to counseling the subject about improving his or her areas of "weakness." What is the intention in focusing upon those weaknesses? The answer is to urge the person closer to the ideal. Both the adviser and the person being advised assume that this the logical thing to do. This, in spite of the fact that the dean of corporate consultants, Peter Drucker, has always advised managers to build on strengths.

There are two difficulties with the process we just described. The first has to do with the idea of improving weaknesses. The second involves the validity of the testing.

Improving Weaknesses

We can applaud anyone's efforts in improving his or her skills. Applying that principle to tennis, we can describe how a weak player has been gradually transformed into a stronger player through good coaching and much practice. We can see the same happening in an organization, where a young but gifted manager, weak in some skills because of inexperience, ends up delivering managerial excellence by focusing on improving in his or her areas of weakness. In both situations the individual is raising skill levels appropriate to the gifts he or she has already been demonstrated to possess.

This is in contrast to personality testing, where factors not appropriate to the individual are artificially made a standard. When this arbitrary standard is applied, everyone will automatically end up with "weaknesses." The result of focusing energy on those so-called weaknesses will probably be that performance in those areas will be built up to a high level of mediocrity. Yet the same amount of energy invested in strengths would pay off in competence and produce enthusiasm in the performer, the manager, and the clients.

Where did this strange concentration on weaknesses come from? It appears to be rooted in the work of the psychiatrists and psychologists, who together are an enormously influential class of people in modern society. In fact, some critics suggest that they are now the high priests of the modern age. Psychiatrists are physicians, and as such they are experts in pathology; that is, they focus upon illness within the personality. They are skilled in looking for weaknesses. This negative preoccupation dominates almost every consideration they make concerning human personality and thinking. Even when dealing with the most positive subject of human action, creativity, they have proposed a number of theories portraying creative urges as necessarily dependent on neurotic preconditioning. This perspective becomes a serious problem when it influences almost every endeavor to assess human personality, even when pathology is irrelevant.

Possessing all the gifts is not a human possibility. Only God can be God. Therefore, it is absurd to discuss the absence of a particular gift in terms of weakness. In fact it is inherent to the nature of man to have limitations. Normal people have limitations. We may not sing like a recording star, but that in no way can be considered a weakness. It is merely something we don't do. We may not be managerial. That is not a weakness either—unless we decide to take a managerial job.

Validity of Personality Tests

Going back to the personality tests that produced this portrayal of strengths and weaknesses, we would ask, *Who represents the perfect standard against which we are being compared? Who is this ideal person? Where is this person?* The answer is that this paragon is not a real person. We living, complex, vibrant human beings are being compared to an academic fiction, something that does not nor can exist. This academic model has nothing to do with personhood nor with reality.

> *Each one should test his own actions. Then he can take pride*
> *in himself, without comparing himself to somebody else,*
> *for each one should carry his own load.*
>
> Galatians 6:4–5 NIV

Does that mean that all tests are wrong? No, it does not. Testing makes sense in the area of skills. It makes sense to use a typing test to find out how fast someone uses the keyboard. It makes sense to use a test to find out if students know their algebra or their spelling. A test is useful wherever there is a positive answer to two questions:

1. Is the information you are seeking measurable?
   How fast? How far? How heavy? How much? How accurate?
2. Is the information you are seeking appropriate?

   An example of "appropriate": Giving high school students a test to determine if they know the traffic laws before granting them drivers licenses.

   An example of "inappropriate": Denying a person a job as a salesman because a test identified the person as an introvert. The category "Introvert" is an irrelevant item of information in a job match, because what might be temperamentally true in a non-motivated situation might not necessarily be true in motivated circumstances.

We can understand that since most people just put up with personality tests, they might not fully appreciate their implications. Familiarity has done us in. Think about what the apostle Paul would have said about

Christians' attempting to measure who makes a good pastor, as has been attempted in some seminaries. Each pastoral candidate is gauged against a standard of leadership so comprehensive no one ever makes the mark. What pastor do you know has all the gifts necessary to be a leader, preacher, shepherd, evangelist, manager, theologian, teacher, church grower, counselor, visionary, trainer, and educator? No wonder we find so many pastors privately agonizing over their inadequacies. No profession on earth has such formidable standards. How does such an approach fit into the apostle Paul's teaching?

There are different kinds of gifts, but the same Spirit.
There are different kinds of service, but the same Lord.
There are different kinds of working, but the same God
works all of them in all men.

1 Corinthians 12:4–6 NIV

It strikes me as curious that out of the thousands and
thousands of factor-analytic studies that smother us today,
scarcely any are carried through in such a manner as to
discover the internal, unique, organizational units that
characterize a single life.

Gordon W. Allport[2]

MINISTRY PARAGONS

When looking at areas of ministry and service, we find that in addition to corporate models of leadership, church and parachurch organizations require a list of additional qualities. These are character traits, such as integrity, honesty, loyalty, faithfulness, obedience, and perseverance, that, in addition to faith, tend to become part of the mix in defining Christian leadership. We believe their addition confuses our understanding of leadership, since they are qualities we would expect of anyone who takes the Christian life seriously, whether or not he or she intends to become a leader. Second, when character is included in the actual definition of leadership, it leaves us unprepared to understand the phenomenon of powerful leaders who clearly have the gifts of leadership but with deficient character.

For example, a principle found in a number of writings on leadership says that a leader cannot expect others to be obedient to his leadership if he has not learned obedience himself. That is good as a principle, but the reality is that there are leaders who are now in strong positions of leadership who know little of obedience in their own lives. So we can conclude that this principle is not an ingredient of leadership per se. It refers to character in leadership, which is entirely different.

We make this separation between factors of character and factors of leadership in order to think clearly, not because there are such neat categories in the actual process of living. This corrects the notion that we can develop leaders merely by developing character. Yet character development is almost the sole leadership training activity in Christian circles. Character development does not produce leaders. We can only get leadership from those God has gifted with leadership capabilities. We can only develop what is already there. We cannot add what God has not installed.

None of this is intended to diminish the importance of character. In fact, we will focus on the subject in a subsequent chapter, because it is crucial. What is intended here is to perceive leadership in terms that make pragmatic sense. We cannot manage character, we can only nurture it. We can, however, manage the development, placement, and strategic use of leaders. Thinking in terms of "the ideal leader" does not help us with such management at all.

EXAMPLES IN THE U.S. PRESIDENCY

The United States presidency is the most powerful leadership position in the world. It would be the logical place to put the ideal leader. After all, there is so much at stake. Yet we have never seen a leader in the White House who even remotely matches the models that have been developed by our culture. President Carter, who was a gifted peacemaker, was an ineffective manager. President Reagan, who had a strong vision, was not always on top of the facts. President Bush, who could unify international leaders, had no vision. Having been taught to expect each new president to be a superman, we have failed to fully appreciate the gifts he does have. We have failed to surround him with people whose gifts will complement his. Without such complementary efforts, every president must end up as a partial success at best. As a consequence, we are not realistic in our evaluations of presidential performance. What is true about presidential leadership is true of our thinking about all leadership.

If we insist on defining leaders in terms of the ideal, we have no process in place whereby we can enhance their success. All we can do is urge them to strive to do better as defined by the ideal and in terms of whatever particular model we find attractive. That is now happening in organizations all over the world. We are waiting for our leaders to be super-leaders and criticize them when they are not. That automatically means that no one quite makes the grade, which breeds dissatisfaction, no matter what excellent results a leader brings about. In the Christian context, this practice has diminished the importance of the functioning body, where each leader is dependent upon the complementary gifts of others. That perspective remains a large emphasis in the New Testament, but a small one in our actual practice. The costs are incalculable.

UNREALISTIC EXPECTATIONS

Working from unrealistic models is normative in organizations of all kinds. The chairman of a search committee for a college president once conferred with us about the particular leader for which they should be looking. We said that we probably knew what kind of person they wanted. "You want a person who has an educational vision, who can manage a large institution, and who can raise money for improvement and expansion."

"Yes," was the response. "That is exactly the kind of person we want. Can you recommend a person like that?"

We didn't think it likely that God made anyone like that. We suggested that they decide which of the three was the priority item, find a candidate very strong in that area, and then develop innovative ways to cover the others. If, for example, money was the most serious concern, they could get a president who had a track record in developing the kinds of funds needed beyond what the director of development would bring in. Then they could complement those gifts with someone to develop the educational vision. That might turn out to be the dean of faculty together with selected faculty, for example. But to seek a candidate who would be outstanding in all three priority activities would probably end up in their hiring Mr. Average, who might be able to do something in each but nothing special in any.

When we are willing to drop the goal of becoming a paragon leader, we will be better able to expand the effectiveness of the gifts we already possess. There is no possibility of our becoming somebody other than who we already are. Let us give up any attempt to become the leaders others may desire or hope for, so we can be the leaders we are gifted to be.

Notes

1. Ayn Rand, *The Fountainhead* (New York: Macmillan, 1985).
2. Gordon W. Allport, *The Person in Psychology* (Boston: Beacon, 1968), 99.

SECTION TWO

THE GIFTS
OF A LEADER

*F*or if the trumpet give an
uncertain sound, who shall
prepare himself to the battle?

1 CORINTHIANS 14:8 KJV

CHAPTER 7

LOOKING AT YOU

How can we know whether we are leaders, and if we are, what kind of leaders we are gifted to be?

In chapter 5 we observed that people do things in their own way and with such determination that we concluded that each person is unique. That means each person is motivated to achieve results that differ from those of anyone else. That includes leadership. Each leader leads in a particular way, and each leader fits only certain situations. We can discover what those particular ways of leading are when we see repeated patterns of behavior from the past.

Our confidence in proposing that each leader leads in a unique fashion is based on extensive work in consulting with thousands of individuals. Professionally, we provide written reports that identify up to sixty gifted elements that make up a portrait of how an individual operates.[1] That information is used to make decisions about careers, ministry, job-fit, placement, selection, team building, education, human resource development, and work relationships.

Our technology is an open system. We do not work within a fixed number of gifts but merely describe what we see. We do not compare an individual to others, nor do we drop him into a box, label him, position him in some kind of grid, measure him, or try to describe him with combinations of limited descriptors. Each new encounter with a person is a fresh beginning. This approach enables us to continually discover new gifts as they appear from time to time in new clients. These additional discoveries occur even though one would assume that, given the numbers, by now we would have encountered every possible combination of gifts. That, of course, seriously underestimates the genius of the One who designed each person.

We have worked with executives, artists, homemakers, pastors, surgeons, engineers, counselors, media people, accountants, actors, scientists, mature adults, and young students. Never have we found anyone duplicate anyone else in terms of his or her giftedness. What we have found, in addition to many other roles, is that certain people are leaders. As we stated in chapter 1, all leaders are similar in that they are change agents. None of them, however, brings about change in the same way or in the same arena. Given this splendid diversity, readers may appreciate why we strongly protest the overuse of leadership models.

Since no leader exactly duplicates another, there is no way to arrive at an absolute number of leadership styles. But, although there is no duplication of leaders, there are enough similarities in leaders for us to organize them into nine Leadership Families. That allows us to demonstrate the nature of different leadership styles and how they may clash with or complement one another. Professionally, we do not use these categories to *identify* leadership styles; we use them to *explain* leadership styles. The leadership style is only part of a larger inventory of gifts, so we encourage spending the time to develop a detailed portrait of your gifts. Instructions can be found in chapter 8.

LEADERSHIP FAMILIES

O n the following page we present an introductory diagram of Leadership Families. It displays three basic families, with two leadership variations for each. After the diagram there are three sections, one for each Leadership Family. Each section opens with a chart outlining the possible characteristics of the leadership style being described. On a facing page that chart is followed by explanations of the leadership style, with examples. That explanation is then followed by descriptions of the leadership style variations. All this material is but a part of a larger gift identification process, the end product of which is The MOTIF Report (referred to by footnote earlier). The Leadership Families are presented for use by the reader but, as copyrighted material, cannot be reproduced by any means without written permission from the author.

LEADERSHIP FAMILIES

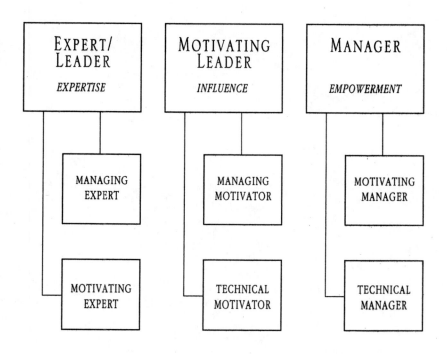

THE EXPERT/LEADER

FEATURING EXPERTISE

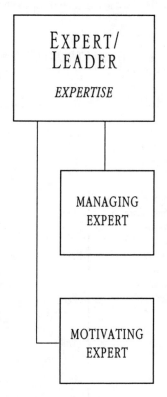

LEADERSHIP STYLE
EXPERT/LEADER

A person who achieves direct results, rather than working through others to get them. Expert/Leaders cause changes or make improvements based on a specialized body of knowledge or technology. They are experts who advance knowledge, skills, or methods. Other specialists may look to them as a resource to learn about new developments or acquire new skills.

EXAMPLES OF GIFTS THAT MAY BE PRESENT IN AN EXPERT/LEADER

STYLE	ROLE	FOCUS	RESULTS
Expert/Leader: exploits personal mastery to make conceptual or technical advances	Researcher Conceptualizer Innovator Problem Solver Developer Maximizer Designer Builder Synthesizer	Technology Synthesis Concepts Process People Systems Information Things/Products Arts Body of Knowledge	Discovery Advance Development Breakthrough Improvement Creation

USING THE LEADERSHIP STYLE CHART

The chart on the opposite page provides four columns. The first column concisely defines the Leadership Family. The three remaining columns provide lists of possibilities for each component. Select one or two items from each list, or substitute words that would provide greater accuracy.

DEFINITIONS

STYLE = The Leadership Family, in this case, Expert/Leader.
Examples for this family would include engineer, theologian, artist, mechanic, surgeon, programmer, sociologist, or physicist, but only those who bring about change, progress, or creativity.

ROLE = The characteristic way the Expert/Leader operates. One or a combination of two items could be selected to provide the most accurate description.
Examples: Innovative Problem Solver, which would mean that this leader is good at dealing with problems that require innovative solutions.

FOCUS = The general subject matter with which the Expert/Leader wants to work.

RESULTS = The kind of changes the Expert/Leader achieves.

EXAMPLES

James D.
STYLE: Expert/Leader
ROLE: Builder
FOCUS: Systems
RESULTS: Improvement

A commercial builder who cut a week off previous schedules by redesigning the logistics of a building project. Keeps looking for ways to enhance efficiency and quality and meet the deadline sooner. Needs to work in an operation large enough to adequately sustain the use of his gifts. A small operation requires the wearing of too many hats. He does not maintain, so he would need to be complemented by a maintaining manager who assures follow-up. He has gained for the company a reputation for bringing projects in on time and within budget.

Janice H.
STYLE: Expert/Leader
ROLE: Developer
FOCUS: Information
RESULTS: Advance

A researcher who provides social action groups with information about emerging regional and national legislation. She keeps those organizations abreast of what might be happening by finding ways to qualify information by assessing the likelihood of proposed legislation becoming law, how much attention an issue is getting, obstacles to passage of legislation, and who the key players are. She needs to be complemented by someone to coordinate the staff. This complement must be able to tolerate the researcher's multiple contacts with staff as she develops new ways to enrich the acquisition of information and the swifter delivery of it. She might tend to restrict clients to those who are dealing with forward-looking issues.

CHARACTERISTICS

Expert/Leaders usually are disinterested in making an impact upon people or leading people, both of which are the only ways most people define leadership. When people do appear in their FOCUS they appear as subject matter, something to be studied, such as people behavior or social behavior. Expert/Leaders become known as leaders because of their level of knowledge. Because they are leaders, they keep pushing their expertise to higher levels and toward new applications. They tend to attract other specialists in their field or from other fields, with whom they share information and new developments or establish mentoring relationships. Expert/Leaders leaders are critical to the advance of knowledge, technology, and wisdom in our organizations.

COMPLEMENTS

Expert/Leaders usually need to be complemented by managers to take care of the follow-up. These managers should be skilled in long-term oversight in

order to balance the project orientation often characteristic of most Expert/
Leaders.

It is a good idea to determine how many balls this kind of leader can jug-
gle. The extremes are:

> Expert/Leaders who tend to be intensely fo-
> cused and in-depth, giving attention to one factor,
> issue, or project at a time
>
> vs.
>
> Expert/Leaders who are so developmental
> they are capable of ending up with too many
> projects

MANAGEMENT

Expert/Leaders usually thrive best where they are given considerable independence. If they are operating on a level where they are being managed, who-
ever does the managing needs to understand that hands-on management is
poison to most Expert/Leaders. They, in turn, usually make poor managers.

THE BEAUTY OF THE EXPERT/LEADER

Expert/Leaders liberate us with stimulating insights and creative approaches. They furnish the mind with new symbols, enabling us to think
thoughts we could not otherwise think. Others gain new knowledge and the
innovations of fresh thinking and doing, while still others expand past discoveries. Expert/Leaders tend to be at the technical cutting edge of our organizations.
When their specialties complement each other (e.g., technical advance with spiritual advance), they are the creative edge of our civilization.

CHARACTER FLAWS

Each leadership style is prone to certain character flaws that in the absence
of vigorous character development are apt to surprise those who assume that
depth in one area of life means depth in all areas of living. Expert/Leaders are so
knowledgeable or are so conceptual that some leaders may display considerable
amounts of arrogance toward the ignorance of others. At their worst, they are
know-it-alls who are blind to other styles of thinking or to the possibility of differing conclusions.

PROBLEMS IN ORGANIZATIONS RELATING TO THE EXPERT/LEADERS

CHURCH—Today's church is in dire need of certain Expert/Leaders to transform the content of a Christian culture that is generally imitative, uncreative, and desperately ineffective in addressing a degenerating secular society. Permeated by a culture too dependent upon the exercise of political rather than spiritual power, churches do not understand how to bring transformation. The Expert/Leader who understands this would be an excellent complement and mentor to any of the influential leaders.

BUSINESS—Business is dependent upon Expert/Leaders to stay competitive. The problem for business is an inability to distinguish Expert/Leaders (who deal with technical advance) from experts (who deal with technology), because they both rarely look like any of the leadership models business is used to. In addition, business is not very good at managing innovative or creative people.

SCHOOLS—Granting some excellent exceptions, schools tend to focus on institutional survival. When creativity and innovation do appear, they are confined to the classrooms, safely distant from the administration and management of the school. Appropriate Expert/Leaders, combined with visionary leaders, are needed to assist in the redefining of the content and purposes of education, especially now, when so many schools are being controlled by administrators and bureaucratic committees.

VARIETIES OF EXPERT/LEADERS

Motivating EXPERT

A Motivating Expert works primarily out of technical or conceptual know-how but is also motivated to make an impact upon other leaders, professionals, or upon entire organizations in order to stimulate technical progress or conceptual advances. This is a leader who not only is influential, but who may be found displaying expertise through various media, someone who is always causing learning, discussion, or the upgrading of skills to take place in others, one who eagerly interfaces with specialists from other fields of study. Such a leader is able to effectively introduce new ideas to fellow specialists or to organizations who need them or who need to be made aware of needing them. Essentially, these leaders are a useful interface between people and a body of knowledge or technology.

Examples:

- The engineer who influences his firm into upgrading its technical support systems
- The theologian who gets involved in the development of public policy
- The educator who is motivated to speak for educational change before a political committee

Managing EXPERT

A Managing Expert primarily works with technical or conceptual skills but is also able to manage others. The management most often involves project management, enabling a variety of technical or conceptual specialists to function effectively together. Where the management gifts are especially strong, supervision of a research facility, as a stage for creative or developmental technical advances, is appropriate.

Examples:

- The electronics engineer who engages experts from other technical fields to develop a breakthrough in the design of computer screens

- The journalist who develops a staff of writers for a new publication
- The pastor who draws people through preaching and also is strong in working through other leaders to get results
- The counselor who directs a TV production on relationships

THE MOTIVATING LEADER

FEATURING INFLUENCE

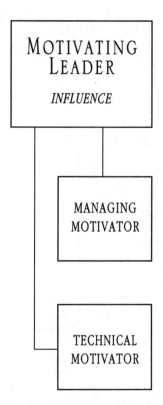

LEADERSHIP STYLE
MOTIVATING LEADER

A Motivating Leader influences people to change their actions or attitudes or degree of involvement or commitment.

EXAMPLES OF GIFTS THAT MAY BE PRESENT IN A MOTIVATING LEADER

STYLE	ROLE	FOCUS	RESULTS
Motivating Leader: exploits own personality to change people			
	Persuader		
	Supporter		
	Inspirer		
	Guide		
	Recruiter		
	Instigator		
	Visionary		
	Crusader		
	Pioneer		
	Advocate		
	Ambassador	Individuals	
		Groups	
		Teams	
		Audiences	
		Company	
		Constituency	
		Organizations	
			People who are:
			Multiplied
			Convinced
			Redirected
			Changed
			Involved
			Committed
			Motivated
			Recruited
			Converted
			Mobilized

USING THE LEADERSHIP STYLE CHART

The chart on the opposite page provides four columns. The first column concisely defines the Leadership Family. The three remaining columns provide lists of possibilities for each component. Select one or two items from each list, or substitute words that would provide greater accuracy.

DEFINITIONS

STYLE =   The Leadership Family, in this case, Motivating Leader.
          Examples include pastors, certain consultants, actors, public speakers, recruiters, lobbyists, evangelists, politicians, TV and radio commentators, columnists, ambassadors, educators.

ROLE =   The characteristic way the Motivating Leader operates. One or a combination of two items could be selected to provide the most accurate description. Use a dictionary to clarify your understanding of these roles.
          Example: Supporting/Recruiter, a leader who recruits people to be involved but goes beyond this first stage to support the individual as he or she gets integrated into the organization.

FOCUS =   The general subject matter with which the Motivating Leader wants to work.

RESULTS = The kind of changes the Motivating Leader achieves.

EXAMPLES

> Lynn T.
> STYLE: Motivating Leader
> ROLE: Recruiter
> FOCUS: Individuals and Groups
> RESULTS: Convinced and Involved

Lynn is highly successful in getting rural, black Americans registered to vote. She engages people by getting them to talk about themselves, their hopes, and their problems. She takes the time to explain how each person makes a difference in solving those difficulties common to the whole community. She convinces people to begin participating by voting. She then follows up by keeping them informed about the issues, getting neighborhood groups together to discuss them, and seeing if there is any possibility of coming to a consensus.

> Stan R.
> STYLE: Motivating Leader
> ROLE: Guide
> FOCUS: Teams
> RESULTS: Involved, Mobilized

A director of marketing for a company that achieves goals by putting together teams of specialists. He empowers his team to figure out the best way to achieve marketing objectives. Being a guide, he doesn't take a strong, visible presiding role but inserts the appropriate amount of guidance for the team, given its degree of diversity and the particulars of the goal. When his department encounters obstacles, he mobilizes a task force and attacks the problems almost with military fervor. Employees are at a loss to describe his leadership style, since he is gentle and almost invisible when facilitating a team, but highly aggressive in battle when he is seen charging at an obstacle with his task force running with him.

CHARACTERISTICS

Motivating Leaders are the closest to what most people expect leaders to look like. That is because many of them are highly visible, in the limelight, appearing before audiences or persuading groups. Since all their activities involve people, all Motivating Leaders are visible to some degree and quite relational, though often with audiences and groups and not individuals, which can be confusing to those who expect the energy displayed on the stage to transfer to a one-on-one encounter. In contrast to Expert/Leaders, who are involved with a particular body of knowledge or expertise, Motivating Leaders, although they are likely to operate out of some subject matter or issue, are really applying the energy of their personalities to create changes or to advance a cause. They do a lot of talking. In contrast to the Expert/Leader, who concentrates on the technology with which he or she is working and who expects conclusions to be arrived at through the language of technology or art, the Motivating Leader expects people to capitulate to or make a decision based on his or her influence.

COMPLEMENTS

Clearly, the Motivating Leader tends to make an impact and once that is achieved, moves on to the next opportunity. When Motivating Leaders get caught up in an issue or crusade, they tend to build up momentum without much consideration for its impact upon staff or resources. If they are in key leadership roles, they are best complemented by feasibility managers. The more a Motivating Leader operates in a professional role the less difficulty there is for him. The more he is involved with top leadership positions, the greater the need for complementary supporting leadership teams to be built around him.

MANAGEMENT

Motivating Leaders usually want as much independence as possible to influence others their way, so they prefer to skirt around management. Managers are, however, a boon to this kind of leader because they keep an eye on the long-terms goals and make sure that the results being achieved by the Motivating Leader fit those goals. Motivating Leaders usually need to get responses from their managers about the quality of their work. Motivating Leaders are not, themselves, typically good managers.

THE BEAUTY OF THE MOTIVATING LEADER

Motivating Leaders as a class of leaders are highly attractive, whether working in the backwoods of the deep South or before TV cameras. They tend to focus upon people, engaging them and taking care of a basic human need—the need for attention—in a highly energetic way. Some Motivating Leaders are gifted to see and articulate a vision for organizations and and communities. That is something without which no civilization can survive.

Motivating Leaders charm us, cajole us, or intimidate us to get us going. Where projects are dying or people are losing interest, they revive and motivate. They call for commitments and get them. They call us to the battlefield, and we fight for a cause. They display the flash of energy peculiar to human personalities and remind us of the beauty of who we are.

CHARACTER FLAWS

Each leadership style is prone to certain character flaws. Motivating Leaders are able to use their personalities as tools to bring about change in people.

Therefore, their role in making the impact is often of greater importance than the content of the message itself. With this emphasis, such a leader may not find it difficult to exploit the facts even to the point of distortion in some cases. They can tend to promise things that have not been approved by those who actually have to deliver, creating problems about follow-up. Motivating Leaders who are gifted to be in the spotlight need to caution themselves about what are popularly referred to as ego trips, decidedly a hurdle in attempting to achieve any level of humility.

PROBLEMS REGARDING MOTIVATIONAL LEADERS IN ORGANIZATIONS

CHURCH—There isn't another organization that provides so many opportunities for Motivational Leaders as does the church. This has been especially true as the majority of contemporary churches have moved from supportive leadership to highly visible leadership. The danger is the tendency to give too much authority to the highly visible leaders and thereby converting congregations to audiences or distorting ministries so that they become lopsided crusades.

BUSINESS—Business makes wide use of Motivational Leaders on all levels, but businesses repeatedly make a mistake that is very costly, yet hard to detect until it's too late. That mistake is to assume that Motivational Leaders are Managers because they engage people so strongly and often display clear qualities of leadership. Time and time again we discover Motivational Leaders in positions that must be occupied by Managerial Leaders if we are genuinely interested in profits, which is what business is all about. Another problem is that companies assume every leadership position requires a Manager, when sometimes what is needed is a Motivator or Recruiter. When it comes to management, do not expect people who naturally focus on their own performance, whether as Expert/Leaders or Motivating Leaders, to take an intense interest in facilitating the success of others.

SCHOOLS—Generally, Motivational Leaders who are teachers tend to put a higher priority on students than on subject matter. This is especially fitting in grade schools. Too often such Motivational Teachers, because they tend to stand out, are encouraged to get into administration. This means losing a good teacher and gaining a mediocre administrator.

Another problem is that the title Administration in education usually covers the maintaining functions of administration plus the provision of educational leadership. This is not at all successful, since in most educational settings the first dominates the second, leaving the public schools of our nation without the drive and the vision to tackle the formidable problems they face. There are people who can solve these problems, but Administration, which has the power to initiate change, is usually inclined toward bureaucracy. Educational bureaucracies do not tolerate change-agents very well.

VARIETIES OF EXPERT/LEADERS

Managing MOTIVATOR

A Managing Motivator makes an impact upon people to change their attitudes or behavior or opinions, or to gain acceptance or get involved. This leader can also manage a small staff supporting his or her efforts. An example of such a leader would be a political personality who makes a major impact on the legislative floor, but who also makes sure that there is follow-up with constituencies, that organized legislative projects are brought to conclusion, that the people who make up his staff are doing well, and that he or she is facilitating their success.

Technical MOTIVATOR

A Technical Motivator convinces people to change their attitudes, or gains acceptance or gets involvement in a project where a particular body of knowledge, technical experience, credential, or demonstrated skill is necessary to bring about progress.

Examples:

- The physician who can convince primitive tribal chiefs to accept vaccinations
- The salesperson who can get a business to accept and buy a new computer system
- The city planner who can convince city agencies to adapt an extensive plan for urban renewal

Technical Motivators are similar to Motivating Experts in that they both influence others concerning their area of knowledge or technology. Selection would depend upon where the emphasis is to be weighted. Technical Motivators would emphasize those being influenced and Motivating Experts the specified technology.

Purely technical associates might be irritated with the emphasis of Technical Motivators, believing that a preoccupation with impressing people is capable of compromising technical depth. Laypeople, however, would have the reverse view. They would appreciate the Technical Motivator's ability to communicate complex ideas in a way that they can understand. Therefore, the Technical Motivator usually makes a good teacher and is willing to sacrifice being at the cutting edge of technology to bring students to an appreciation of it.

THE MANAGER

EMPOWERING PEOPLE

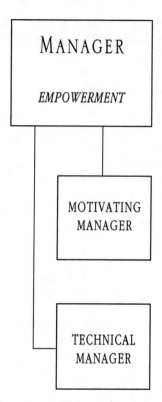

LEADERSHIP STYLE
MANAGER
⟨◦⟫

A Manager works through people to get appropriate results within the constraints of time and resources. The Manager sustains progress until the goals are achieved.

EXAMPLES OF GIFTS THAT MAY BE PRESENT IN A MANAGER

STYLE	ROLE	FOCUS	RESULTS
Managing Leader: applies authority to direct or to empower others to get results	Overseer Monitor Supervisor Director Orchestrator Chairman Presider Participator Facilitator	Individuals Groups Teams Volunteers Organizations Experts	Growth New Development Predetermined Goals

USING THE LEADERSHIP STYLE CHART

The chart on the opposite page provides four columns. The first column concisely defines the Leadership Family. The three remaining columns provide lists of possibilities for each component. Select one or two items from each list, or substitute words that would provide greater accuracy.

DEFINITIONS

STYLE =   The Leadership Family, in this case, Manager.

Managerial leadership is carried out in many different roles, on many organizational levels, and in all kinds of organizations, but always involves working through people to make things happen to achieve goals.

ROLE =   The characteristic way the Manager operates.

Role Definitions:

Overseer—A manager who is on-site to survey the action and to examine the results to be sure they meet specifications. Emphasis is on the final product.

Monitor—A manager who stays close to the operation to regulate the processes. Emphasis is on procedure.

Supervisor—A manager who directs a course of action. Emphasis is on team effectiveness.

Director—A manager of an effort requiring many independent professionals. Emphasis is on control.

Orchestrator—A manager who blends the efforts of simultaneous professionals into a cohesive whole. Emphasis is on vision.

Chairman—A manager who brings the key players together periodically to assure operation is on track. Emphasis is on responsibility.

Presider—A manager who acts as president or moderator. Emphasis is on authority.

Participative Manager—A manager who leads the team into action in which he or she also participates. Emphasis is on action.

Facilitative Manager—A manager who focuses on individual success and provides training and resources to equip his people to get results, and who supports them until they do. Emphasis is on support.

FOCUS = The general subject matter with which the Manager wants to work. In the case of the Manager, the subject is the people through whom the results will be attained.

RESULTS = What the Manager achieves. These are the predetermined goals of the organization. Many, if not most, leaders who are Managers tend to maintain an organization to keep it running effectively and reach predetermined goals. However, they cause others to take action to do so. They work through people.

Other Managers go beyond maintaining the operation to bring about changes in their department or group. These changes may mean greater effectiveness in how they get results, or they may mean advancing new developments in their area of expertise. In manufacturing, for example, the changes might involve finding a more productive way to run the organization all the way to actually redesigning it.

CHARACTERISTICS

When considering the nature of managerial leadership, we must differentiate between managerial gifts and positions in organizations that are designated managerial. There are many with the title of manager without the abilities of Manager. They are often Professional Leaders who are expected to transfer their high level of performance in their field of expertise to performing as a manager. This is an unhappy situation if the new position actually requires managerial actions. A common example of this is where a high performing salesperson is promoted to Sales Manager in the hope that his or her selling gifts will thereby be transferred to the entire sales force.

Managers and Motivating Leaders are similar in that they both focus on people, in contrast to Expert/Leaders, who get directly involved with the work. However, Managers work through others to get results, whereas Motivating Leaders make an impact upon others as the result. Managers provide sustained leadership, whereas Motivating Leaders move on once the impact is achieved. The Manager brings shape and order to the efforts of others and is key to liberating the gifts of employees to achieve the goals.

COMPLEMENTS

A Manager often has administrative abilities, but the emphasis is on people. Therefore, when the size of a project or the department or organization gets large enough to require extensive administration, the General Manager needs to then be complemented with an administrator who can stay on top of the day-to-day operation. Frequently, the Manager also needs to be complemented by Professional Leaders who can match the progress of the Manager with equally progressive technology. Sometimes that can be adequately achieved through technical consultants.

Managerial gifts seldom combine with the gifts of visionary leadership. That means that a Manager in the position of president or director of an organization is a problem for those organizations which need more than the advice of consultants to forge and communicate a vision for the future.

MANAGEMENT

Managers are best managed by those who give authority with responsibility plus the freedom to fully use their leadership gifts. Managers who report to vice-presidents need to be aware that vice-presidents generally are involved with a particular technology, such as advertising, marketing, or finance, and as such are not necessarily gifted as Managers. They may think nothing of getting involved with a Manager's department without going through the Manager. In such cases it is a wise procedure to discuss the harmonies and potential clashes of differing styles. In fact, such a discussion is best held before problems arise and create unnecessary bad feelings.

THE BEAUTY OF THE MANAGER

Managers, or the lack of them, are behind the success or failure of every organization. No organization can accomplish anything without people, and it is the Manager who gets those people to work effectively as an organization. Select Managers who are gifted to take on the required role, and we are assured of excellence.

CHARACTER FLAWS

Managers need to be disciplined in their use of authority. Our culture generally distorts our understanding of authority by treating it as a badge of success. Wise Managers will fend off the temptation to treat authority as an indicator of worth and will instead apply it only to support employees.

Problems Regarding Managerial Leaders in Organizations

CHURCH—Churches have been challenged for years to get the laity into the action. It not only makes sense in terms of efficiency but is also a scriptural requirement. Pastoral training and books on the subject have had marginal impact upon the church. That is because pastors rarely have the gifts of the Manager and have not recognized the critical need for them. Managers are the only people who can move the people out of pews and get them into the action and *keep them in action*.

BUSINESS—It is odd that we live in an age where technically we can place a person on the moon with precision, but placing people in the right position in an organization is a gamble. Business needs to seriously critique its own assumptions about leadership, to say nothing about the Manager. There is someone out there who is gifted to cure any problem or pull off any results business can name. The difficulty is that businesses are imprecise in finding such people and in managing them.

SCHOOLS—Unlike business, schools need to evaluate how much their style as an institution is expressed in terms of being a community. If being a learning community is a serious component of the educational vision, the manner in which management is executed needs to be periodically examined to make sure it enhances community rather than erodes it. The fastest way to find that reality is to ask students and teachers. The ultimate in educational management is when it gets rave reviews from the community it serves. Too often, it is seen as an impediment.

VARIETIES OF EXPERT/LEADERS

Motivating MANAGER

Motivating Managers work primarily through people to get a result, ensuring follow-up and working within the constraints of the available resources, but they are also able to make a strong impact upon others through the style of their personalities. This might be expressed by influencing a team to enhance production beyond previous standards, by establishing favorable relationships between departments, or by lobbying for more resources to develop new ventures. Rarely does the influencing portion of a Motivating Manager involve visionary gifts. When it does, such a leader is best placed where he or she can resolve the inherent tension in an organization between managerial needs and visionary necessity.

Technical MANAGER

Technical Managers work primarily through people to get a result, ensuring follow-up and working within the constraints of the available resources. They can do so in a technical setting or in a situation where a particular body of knowledge or technical experience is necessary to bring about required results. These are the kind of managers who are in the action with the team, who gain respect because of their expertise in addition to managing. Manager Experts are similar to Technical Managers because they combine technical know-how with managerial abilities, so both would be good project managers. Selection would be dependent upon the emphasis, the former where the weight of the responsibility is on expertise, the latter where the size of the project places the emphasis on management. Reverse the roles and the results will be painful for the organization.

Note

1. The technology used is MOTIF®. It is a nontest, nonpsychoanalytical inventory of the subject's strengths, based on achievement history and used for purposes of career development, management, and human resource development. Copyright © 1988, by Ralph T. Mattson.

CHAPTER 8

―――――○*ЛШП*○―――――

DISCOVERING
GIFTS

Any attempt to measure the gifted distinctives of an individual is like putting calipers to love. When we perceive the distinctives of a person's gifts we are encountering an immeasurable wonder. It is a world of its own. This is as true for a struggling grade school student as it is for the inventor of the computer chip.

> *If I want to know a person, what is the best way to go about doing it? And now I can rephrase this question more pointedly. How good for this purpose are the usual procedures of normal physical sciences (which, remember, is the widely accepted paradigm for all the sciences and even for all knowledge of any kind)? In general my answer is that they are not very good at all. As a matter of fact, they are practically useless if I want not only to know about you but also to understand you.*
>
> Abraham H. Maslow[1]

Our culture does not have a rich language for describing the mystery of human intentionality and its capability of thrusting a thought into the realm of action. Yet every object in our environment has had its origin in the life of a person's will. In fact, gifts could be described as the product of willfulness. All that is far removed from the modern world of tests and measurements. In the realm of selfhood we cannot justify the assessment tools with which so many of our institutions are preoccupied and to which so many people willingly submit, as if human beings were being stamped out like so many coins at a mint and all we had to do is identify their denomination. What an impoverished language our scientists and politicians have constructed to define us. How meager is our modern understanding of human dignity. How immense the contrast between how we have been taught and what has been portrayed by those who wrestled with the author of human dignity.

Thou it was who didst fashion my inward parts; thou didst
knit me together in my mother's womb. I will praise thee, for
thou dost fill me with awe; wonderful thou art, and
wonderful thy works. Thou knowest me through and
through: my body is no mystery to thee, I was secretly
kneaded into shape and patterned in the depths of the earth.
                                                          Psalm 139:13-14 NEB

In a previous chapter we observed how differently people responded to a specific learning requirement, the requirement that they acquire computer skills. We discovered that each person learned in a different way and for differing reasons. What we did in that chapter was to apply some techniques from the journalist's craft of gathering descriptive facts without any attempts to impose personal interpretations. In the situation we described, everyone was forced to acquire a particular skill. If we step outside such required conditions and observe what a person chooses to do, we discover a world like no other. It is a world of detailed action and rich experience. In this case the richness is not necessarily due to drama or prestige or importance from the world's perspective. It is an encounter with the enthusiasm that comes from satisfying achievement, where a person is acting like himself or herself.

Observe what a man does; listen to what he says;
how then can you not know what he is.
                                                          Attributed to Confucius

Let us look at a situation where an individual was crippled by erroneous assumptions about himself, but where listening to the information we elicited from him changed everything. We introduce Steven, who requested support for his decision to leave college in spite of his being an honors student at an Ivy League school. In helping him understand his gifts and his leadership abilities, we encouraged him to tell stories describing times where he brought about certain results that he liked. Then we reflected back, as accurately as possible, the pattern we perceived in the stories he told us. In our report of this meeting with Steven, we will not go into the depth that subsequently followed this initial conversation with him, because we want to point out some immediate high points that reassured Steven of his sanity during his first visit with us.

THE SAGA OF STEVEN

Steven is a college junior from a caring, supportive family. His mother is a teacher and his father a psychiatrist. They are both people-helpers, as are any number of Steven's relatives. Family discussions are riddled with people-behavior talk and supported by a library of people-development books. As a boy, Steven could define an internal conflict before he ever had one. So it is no surprise that he declared psychology as his major at school and counseling as his vocational goal.

We all know that having declared his major and career objective, Steven should have been highly contented. Half the important questions of life were answered for him—and at so young an age. However, even the most perfunctory assessment of Steven's joy would have clearly revealed that he hadn't any. What was wrong?

My name is Steven, and I'm having a tense time in school—in fact, bad enough for me to want to leave, but my parents don't understand why I can't hang on, since I'm in my junior year. I can appreciate why they are upset, but I think my sanity is more important than a degree. Besides, I can always go back later.

What's wrong?

I don't know exactly. I'm confused. I probably should be one of my father's clients. Then he might appreciate what I'm going through.

What do you find yourself thinking about most of the time?

The dreariness of going to school, and if my life is going to be that way forever. I enjoyed high school. I always liked studying and was always pretty much a straight A student. College studies are harder, but they take the same kind of effort . . . but I guess, now, I hate it.

I understand that psychology is your major. How did you select that?

It was easy. My father is a psychiatrist, and my mother a teacher. I know a lot about it. Everyone just assumes that I will either be a counselor or get a doctorate and teach.

I understand that you play basketball. Would professional basketball be attractive to you as a career goal?

I would love it. That would be great. But though I'm really good, I'm not that good.

So you are able to project yourself into the future and imagine yourself playing the game and enjoying it as a profession?

Yes, that's easy to do.

Since you have no trouble using your imagination that way, it seems that whether you look at a counseling career or a basketball career, in either case you can contrive a clear picture in your mind of fit or misfit.

Yes.

It isn't a matter of your not knowing what a counselor does.

Definitely.

So have you imagined what you will be doing, given your career goals? Can you see what it looks like?

I never had to figure that out, because I already am a psychology major and do very well in those courses.

Are you telling me that you will become whatever the school trains you to become?

Only if I can do well in it. I don't believe that someone who has a hard time in taking the kind of courses I take could become good in the profession for which those courses prepare you.

You are assuming that doing well in the training one gets for a profession necessarily means doing well in the profession. I don't find that to be true.

You're telling me that all my high grades in my major aren't evidence that I will do well in counseling or teaching?

That's right. I'll give you an example. Are you very competitive in the way you play basketball?

Yes, I guess I am.

Is it possible that you are competitive in getting high grades?

Yes, I have fun beating everybody out.

If you took a course in Spanish history, do you think you might get a high grade?

I know I would.

Does that mean you want to be a historian?

No, it means I want to get a high grade. I see what you mean. You think I'm a psychology major because of the influences of my family and that I'm getting high grades because I always compete.

I wouldn't make any decisions based on that impression, but it does sound like a good possibility. What do you think?

It makes a lot of sense, but I've never thought of anything else but psychology. The whole department expects me to do great work. I can't imagine what else to do. It looks like I end up with two problems instead of one. If I'm not going to be a psychology major, what am I going to do? At least I had a career goal. If I give it up, what then?

But you have already decided to give it up. You want to leave school.

I guess I sound crazy. You're right. Well, one thing is clear. I sure am confused. Where do we go from here?

Let's put the problem aside for a few minutes. Let's go at this in a different way and find out about you as you are now, before we talk about your future.

This sounds familiar. That's what my parents would do. But I already know about myself.

What do you know?

Well, for starters, I know I am an extrovert.

What can you do with that information? Is the solution to a school and career problem solved by this bit of information about yourself?

I guess not. How about the fact that I'm afraid of snakes?

I guess now we know you shouldn't become a herpetologist.

How about the fact that I like working with people? Now that I think of it, that is one of the reasons I think I should stay in my major.

The question is, what you want to do with people? Impress them? Lead them? Change them? Help them? Teach them? There are all kinds of careers that involve people. Perhaps you are just sociable.

Let's go after other information. For now let's put aside psychological information, traits, great experiences, and temperaments. We need something simpler and more objective. Let's see you in action. Rather than talk *about* you, let's talk *you.* Tell me some stories about times where you've done things you like doing. Start as early as you can remember.

I can remember collecting baseball cards as a kid. I traded a lot. When I traded, I always ended up with more than the guy I traded with. I liked talking a friend into giving up something I wanted for one of my duplicate cards.

How did you do that?

I would keep his attention on the card he wanted instead of what I wanted. That almost always worked.

What did you like most about that?

I had more good cards than anyone else.

Have another example?

Definitely. I remember my first lemonade stand. I set it up one summer on Main Street and charged a nickel a glass. I made pretty good money for a kid. In fact, it went so well that the following summer I set up one on each side of the street and had my brother operate one and I the other. That really was fun. I paid my brother three cents for each glassful he sold. The hard part was keeping track of his sales. I frisked him at the end of the day to make sure we had all the money. I sure did like adding up the profits.

Have another item?

My newspaper route. Did I love that route!

What did you love about it?

The fact that I made it much larger than when I started.

How did you do that?

I usually had one or two leftovers at the end of the route, and I would pick a likely neighbor who wasn't getting the paper and give it to him for a week. At the end of the week I'd ask if he would like to continue getting the paper. He usually did. When I was collecting, I would usually ask people who lived near subscribers if they would like to get the paper. Actually, I wouldn't ask. I would kind of tell them they should have it. "You really need the newspaper," I would say. "When do you want to begin?" I got a lot of new subscribers that way.

Tell me something you liked doing during your high school years.

It's like the newspaper route. I remember how much I liked the magazine drive we had in my junior year. It was great. I was on the committee to figure out a way for our class to make money, and I remembered my friend, who went to another school, told me about the money they made in a magazine drive. There's a company that gives you a percentage of all the subscriptions. In addition, the student that gets the most subscriptions gets a prize, so we did it, and I ended up winning.

How did you get all the subscriptions?

I hit my relatives to begin with, then I systematically went door to door through my neighborhood and sold them. I asked them what magazines they already had and whether they would like to help the junior class by just renewing. Then I'd ask about any new ones they might want. I sold a lot that way.

What did you like about that?

Getting people to buy, seeing the list of subscribers get longer and longer.

Anything you like doing in college?

I like getting the best grades. I like the job I have at the co-op. Started working there in my freshman year and liked it a lot, so I continued. This year I was promoted to sales manager, and have already gone beyond last year's sales target. I get my salespeople all charged up so they really can sell. I don't keep students who just wait for customers to come to them. I get those who are aggressive. It pays.

I think we have enough to at begin solving your problem.

What's the solution?

Think about what you just talked about. All of it is the same in its essentials. Can you see that?

Selling, I guess. You think I should be a salesman?

It looks as if you have an ability to sell. But if you look at all of what you told me, it appears quite entrepreneurial to me. You always end up with more, whether it's money, or baseball cards, or subscriptions. You figure out what kinds of activities have the potential for making money. Then you set it up. None of the achievement activities you talked about display even a hint of helping people with their problems or dealing with concepts of human behavior. No wonder you are miserable as a psychology major.

Do you think I should become a business major?

It looks probable, but we would not make such an important decision based on this short interview. This is rather a quick introduction to relieve the pressure you are feeling, and it is enough for you to see that you are not dealing with some mysterious neurosis. You are naturally disturbed because your career selection is not going to call on the gifts you love to use. Solving psychological problems is not motivating for you. If you think about all the years one spends in a profession, this can look like a disaster.

You make a lot of sense to me. I'm relieved to know that there is a way to go at this, but if you had asked me, I would have told you about some of my counseling sessions in psychology lab. My prof said they were good.

Sure, but then you would be responding to what I led you into, not what you would spontaneously select out of what you liked doing. In the kind of interview one uses in counseling, the counselor often pursues whatever is going to relate to theory. In our case, you had to decide for yourself what was satisfying and where you did well. You were free to talk about anything you wanted as long as it was an achievement that you liked. The next step is to go through a more thorough process. On the basis of the information we will discover, you can consider whatever career will call on the gifts you have.

THE BASIC QUESTIONS

The above dialogue illustrates how we can get information out of the past that displays a pattern of giftedness. The first step requires the development of detailed information based on historical occurrences in a person's life in which specific results were achieved. The second step is to review the information and look for consistent patterns of gifted behavior. The third step is to organize the information so that it provides a portrait of how the individual operates. That can be done by answering the three basic questions.

1. What got the person involved in the action?
2. With what was the person working?
3. What results were achieved by the person?

Answering those questions for Steven looks like the following. The conclusions are based on the above interview plus a subsequent interview. Remember that all of the answers are based on the evidence of repeated behavior.

Steven

1. What gets Steven involved in the action?

Steven is triggered by entrepreneurial opportunities. Whereas some people take action by responding to a need or perhaps a challenge, Steven looks around for opportunities to get more out of less. Clearly he is an example of an emerging young leader who has the ability to identify potential, initiate action from scratch, or radically improve a preexisting operation.

2. With what does Steven work?

He likes to get people into the action and manage them. He gives them enough freedom to get results. He will maximize their effectiveness like he maximizes sales and an increase in his baseball collection as a child. He also works with the details and numbers that give a picture of what is happening, and is gifted to keep a number of balls in the air while his eye is on the goal. Once he achieves the goal, he sets an even higher target or looks for a new venture.

3. What results does Steven bring about?

Steven wants to bring in more sales, or to maximize results or establish a new operation that has potential to grow. He is not a maintaining manager, so he needs to move on to new opportunities when a project reaches maximum growth.

THE BASIC LEADERSHIP QUESTIONS

The same process of gathering information and looking for patterns can be used in discovering an individual's leadership style. The questions used to organize the resulting conclusions correspond to the Leadership Family charts.

1. What leadership role is evident?
2. Upon what does the leader focus?
3. What changes were brought about by the leader?

Examples can be drawn from the Leadership Family Charts.

As you can see from Steven's interview, when Steven responded to the expectations of his family, he became confused. That is easy to understand. They were very supportive and nurtured Steven's outgoing, interesting personality. Their opinions were important to him. However, it wasn't until he told the stories of what he liked doing that we discovered who he really was in terms of his gifts. If he had continued to pursue what his family assumed was fine for him, as it was for them, he would have been in a sadly inappropriate career.

That is why all students should put aside career decisions until they know what they bring to the world of work through their gifts. We need to know who and what we are designed to be before we look at where that fits best as workers or as leaders. God has designed us in a particular way, and we need to follow the call of who He made us to be rather than the call of other influences.

LEADERS AND PEOPLE

Leaders everywhere are hampered by their misunderstanding of people. Given that their primary occupation is to lead people, how they define them is no small matter. Christian leaders should have their thinking tempered by a biblical perspective, but theology is one thing and practice is another. Given the fact that contemporary Christian culture is dominated by the imitative rather than the creative, Christian leaders tend to duplicate the mistakes of the corporation. We are repeatedly surprised by the inordinate respect Christian leaders have for secular people-systems. Given these conditions, the following is aimed at stimulating a different perspective.

> But to each one of us grace has been given as Christ apportioned it. This is why it says:
>
> > "When he ascended on high,
> > he led captives in his train
> > and gave gifts to men."
> > *(Ephesians 4:7–8)*

A study of Ephesians 4 can be a remarkable experience because it connects gifts to matters of the cosmos, the uncreated to the created and the eternal to time. We know gifts are not incidental to the fabric of our relationship to God. In the church we have not only natural gifts, but also spiritual gifts. Some have placed these in opposition to each other, but though the flesh and the Spirit are often in contention, the truth is that God is the only one who could create any gift, whatever category in which we might place it.

The early church did not use tests to determine spiritual gifts. When the apostle Paul was asked how the church could know when someone had the gift of prophecy, his answer was very practical. He said that the church should let someone prophesy if he felt led to do so. Then if the prophecy turned out to be true, the church would know the speaker had the gift of prophecy. Apparently room was given to try out one's gifts. If there was a pattern of success, then they could identify the gifts.

With natural gifts, the same procedure should be taking place in our families as we see our children displaying patterns of behavior. Our society has taught us that such behavior is merely incidental to the development of the child. Although some of it is exactly that, long-term patterns of positive behavior are resources to parents, who can see in them the emerging gifts of their children. They can then affirm and nurture what they see. With such a background, our sons and daughters would know and enjoy who they are and not become victimized by secular systems requiring narrow-minded conformity.

After taking thousands of people through the gift-discovery process, we have discovered that people not only have a clear set of gifts, but those gifts are complex enough to fit more than one job. There are usually a couple of excellent career options based on one's gifts. We may choose between these fitting options because of preference or values. Perhaps conditions will tilt us one way or another: "One option allows me to stay where I am, the other requires me to move to a big city. I don't want to move to a big city." Or maybe values will be the determiner: "I want to contribute to the impact of God's kingdom on contemporary society, so I want to work with an organization that is concerned with those goals."

THE NATURE OF GIFTS

When Steven was being questioned about his achievement activities, he talked about his baseball card collection, basketball, and a lemonade stand. Those all meant something to him, but not because he was taught to like those things. Very often people talk about achievement activities in which they had no prompting or training and sometimes no support from their parents. For example, as a child, I had a strong interest in nature, especially in animal and insect life. No one in my family appreciated my hobby, especially after having to adjust to a couple of small lizards living freely on the window curtains in my room, where they could snatch flies bumping against the window panes. My interests definitely were not encouraged, yet they prevailed. Why? Because there was an inherent, internal disposition to be interested in the complexities of creation, which has lasted to this day.

It may be that some relative bequeathed that interest to me by way of genetics and that gifted interests are a composite of whatever our bloodlines give us. Perhaps it all comes about in the same way as do our looks. But one thing is sure, *we are not interested in everything; we are only interested in certain things.* When others direct our attention to a subject that is of interest to them, we may, out of a desire to please, adapt their subject matter for ourselves. As soon as it is no longer the means through which we get that person's attention, we will discover that our interest wanes. Subjects and activities that are naturally part of our make-up, however, will continue to fascinate us.

> *I don't choose to like the things I like.*
> *I am obliged to like them.*
>
> Picasso

Picasso's statement is especially interesting given the paradox of God's sovereignty and the fact that we can make spontaneous decisions. On one hand we are free to like or be drawn to certain things and ignore others. But it is clear to us that this is not some chaotic capability in which anything can happen. To be free to choose requires a limitation of options out of which we will make our choice. Certain options attract us because they correspond to who we are gifted to be. Not only do we choose what fits us, we seem to have a happy obligation to do so, even to the point of expecting others to like what we like.

GIFTS ARE CONSISTENT

Gifted behavior is consistent behavior. We will not do anything by choice that is not consistent with who we are by nature. This is a wonderful idea when we realize that it describes the reality of a style. Out of the pattern of our past we can make good decisions about the future.

There are people who dislike that idea. They keep saying that we can become anything we want to be, as if all options would occur to everyone. That may sound good, but the reality is that when anyone makes a decision, he considers only certain options in which he has an interest. Our decisions have a consistent style about them. We never look at an infinity of possibilities in a situation. We tend to limit our choices. A friend selects what we reject, and we embrace what others never considered.

Forget the idea that we are merely products of what our homes and schools make us to be. Our gifts emerge in spite of training or education, or whether parents nurture or repress. Outside influences certainly make a difference in the process of knowing and appreciating who we are, sometimes to a ruinous degree. They make no difference as to the kinds of gifts we have any more than they can change the color of our eyes. That is why we often find discussions about nature and nurture to be entirely too simplistic. We cannot define human giftedness as a creation of socialization, nor can we expect giftedness to be purely expressed, no matter what kind of developmental environment an individual experiences.

A child who is born with creative abilities, with words and skills to express them but with little interest in physical accomplishments and no competitive characteristics, is not going to be fundamentally changed by a home where everybody is preoccupied with athletic prowess.

Can such a child be turned into a football player? Would Saturday scrimmages and coaching by Dad make a difference? Certainly it would. It would not be unusual to see a son, in his eagerness to please his father, act in a way that he knows will gain a response. But if Dad sets his sights on an athletic career for his son, he is headed for disappointment. When the conditions that encourage nongifted activity disappear, so will the activity. Temporary, conditioned behavior does not change the basic set of gifts that a person possesses.

Baseball players who are naturally motivated by the sport may have fathers whose most competitive athletic activity takes place each evening when they walk the dog. Students who are motivated to learn through studying may stay in school until they have four academic degrees, even if both parents are sure too much reading confuses the brain.

Not only does active, positive influence on the part of parents not generate our gifts, but negative or passive attitudes on the part of others does not affect how we are designed. They probably will make a very large difference to our feelings about ourselves, but not to who we are created to be. They may deflect us to misfit careers, but they do not change the gifts.

GIFTS CAN BE VALIDATED

We can validate our decisions by comparing the pattern of consistency of what we did in the past to what we do today. How we express our gifts now will be with greater skill and knowledge than we could display as children, but they will be the same gifts.[2] Steven's eventual decision to change his focus from people behavior to entrepreneurial development did not require a leap of faith. When he finally made the decision, it was backed up by considerable history. He was being directed by the past onto a path that he could easily justify. There were no longer any confused, tentative qualities about his decision. He could see it clearly, so it was almost like pressing the "total" key on the calculator.

If we can see ten or twenty years of our being motivated in the context of a team, we can trust that fact and believe we fit teams. We are not going to have a sudden passion for operating as an individualist, no matter what influences come our way. The more our future work can call on the ability to function on a team, the better. It makes common sense.

Perhaps we see years and years of solving problems as a clear characteristic of how we operate. Why not assume that when we figured a way to get out of the playpen, that was a meaningful achievement? That when we got high marks in school whenever we took a test that concentrated on word problems, that meant something. That when the family car was stalled on a highway and we got it to operate again, that revealed something. We can trust the pattern of our past.

One reason we do not, as individuals, see this natural flow of the past in order to understand our future is because we are brought up in a society that, for the most part, does not see the connection. If it did, it would encourage the observation of behavior with other motives than pathological interests. Teachers would be eager to perceive the beginning evidence of strengths in their students and, together with parents, would help put together a portrait of the students' gifted behavior. The teachers could then affirm students about who they are and help them prepare for what they ought to do in life and teach them according to how they are motivated to learn.

As leaders, we can encourage the people we influence to realize they have been given gifts that already make them somebody. We can help correct the unwholesome influence of a society that has people climbing ladders they should not climb and running races for which they are not designed.

People who are in jobs that do not fit their gifts can have a completely relaxed weekend and wake up exhausted on Monday morning as they contemplate the many hours of uninspired effort and labor that stretches before them. However, one of those same persons might work until 3:00 A.M. on a project that engages his gifts and skills. He seems to have plenty of energy in spite of the sparse amount of sleep. That is the difference that exercising our gifts makes.

We should cooperate with the gifts that reside within. They are like a river that cannot be dammed. When we run with the current of our own abilities, we cooperate with the rightness, the genius, of our own nature. These conclusions should be a warning when we are tempted to occupy positions of leadership that do not fit our gifts. They should also be a warning when we attempt to use people in ways that do not fit who God made them to be. It's like the difference between the use of a two-wheel scooter and a precision sports car. Too many of us look at the people we lead as if we had a garage full of scooters when behind appearances there purrs the quiet hum of precision power.

Notes

1. Abraham H. Maslow, *The Psychology of Science* (New York: Harper & Row, 1966).
2. We have observed a possible exception to this conclusion where aspects of these gifts involving high levels of visionary conceptualization do not display themselves clearly until abstract reasoning matures. This is less the case where visualization can be expressed in media, such as in drawing, painting, or musical composition.

SECTION THREE

THE QUALITY OF LEADERSHIP AND THE CHARACTER OF LEADERS

Character is what you are in the dark.

DWIGHT L. MOODY

Neutral men are the devil's allies.

E. CHAPIN

CHAPTER 9

ACTING
AS LEADERS

The preceding chapters portray the differences between leaders, yet
we have merely displayed the tip of the iceberg. The detail of what
any one person brings to the job and how that interacts with others
is a complex wonder, but it is a wonder for which leaders bear responsibility. That is the subject of the next few pages.

When we know that each person is motivated to operate in a particular way, it opens our eyes to opportunities for improvement on all
levels of any organization. To appreciate how large is this need for improvement, sit in the cafeteria of any organization and listen to the con-
versations. There will be abundant evidence that employees and
volunteers in all kinds of organizations are irritated with leaders who do
not lead, managers who cannot manage, and bosses who wield inappropriate authority and control. This is also occurring in ministry and service
organizations, where such conditions collide with the employer's own
values. Although a portion of these conditions is connected to matters of
character, much of it is due to confusion. When we realize that every
work of value, every product of excellence, can only come from the exer-

cise of gifts, we can see the monumental importance of understanding giftedness. It is key to unraveling confusion, especially in regard to understanding the nature of leadership and the placement of leaders. That responsibility is the subject of this section of the book.

OUR LANDSCAPE

Discovering one's own leadership style has its excitement like discovering a new landscape, only this is interior terrain. It is also a matter of acceptance. We did not create the landscape. We have the gifts we have, and that is what we focus upon. If we observe a river in the landscape, that is a feature we can appreciate but about which no decision need be made. It is simply there. We may have to make decisions if we want to cross it or use it, but whatever decisions we make are circumscribed by the presence of the river. It is like discovering oneself to be male or female. There it is, no vote need be taken, no decision made. However, what we *do* with our sexuality is a decisive matter. Much has been said and written about such decisions because they relate to our character. They relate to ultimate things. Similarly, although there is no decision to be made about the kind of leadership gifts we do or do not have, there are decisions about how our gifts are used. Such choices have far-reaching consequences, which is why we need to consider our motives in how we express our leadership abilities.

OUR MOTIVES

Let us refer again to the story of Adam, Eve, and the Fall. We have already made the point that our fallen state, a condition faithfully described by all our newspapers every day, demoted mankind to a position of ignorance. For each of us, personally, that means ignorance about ourselves. One of the reasons our culture is preoccupied with models of how people should operate is because we do not know ourselves. The information in the model replaces the lack of information about ourselves. Even when selecting a model, we pick whatever sounds convincing, rather than what fits, because we don't know what fits.

This inability to know who we are blocks us from being aware of our intrinsic value and importance. We are ignorant about ourselves and each other. That ignorance places large hurdles in the way of our helping each other to understand who each of is and what we have to give. That ignorance makes us vulnerable to what other people expect us to be, which only adds to the confusion.

Why Is This Confusion So Crippling?

We may attempt to treat this as a light thing, but we cannot. We cannot let it pass as something to which we merely have to adjust. That is because we are social beings, and as social beings we have an absolute need to be affirmed by other individuals in order to become individuals ourselves. Such affirmation process begins for all of us as infants, which is why family life is so influential. What the family tells us about ourselves is indelible. Some of us suffer from being told the wrong things about ourselves. Others have been set free by their parents to be what God made them.

That certainly was not a problem for Adam. When he first opened his eyes he beheld his Creator. Adam knew who he was and what he was supposed to do. The One who created him gave him the gifts and the job to be the steward of Eden. Adam had no questions, either, about his identity or about his career. He knew his value, because God Himself said the creation of Adam was good. But mankind lost that knowledge of worth and purpose in the Fall and has been trying to rediscover it ever since.

The Search

Values, which include the importance of God and family in our lives, cannot be assessed merely as a matter of philosophical or theological opinion. They must be addressed in terms of their profound impact upon the very nature of who we are and our capacity to know ourselves. Hearing a teenager sobbing over an attempted suicide triggered by the perceived lack of any significance or meaning is too frequent an occurrence in our time to take any of this lightly. We are made for significance, and too many of us don't know where to find it. And so we become eager participants in a game to demonstrate our importance. One version is to own the kinds of "stuff" that signals our prominence. It's called materialism. Another version of the game is to seek positions of power over others. That is why we may think being a sales manager is more important than being a salesperson, or that being president is more important than being a sales manager. It becomes more a matter of acquiring importance than of job-fit. That is why employees strive to get onto the management track even though most of them do not have a management bone in their bodies. That is why managers strain to climb the management ladder as high as they possibly can, even if they have to hurt others on the way. They climb until they gain their highest level of incompetence. No wonder Jesus Christ said that, in the end, the first shall be last.

Being a leader is good if you have the God-given gifts for leadership. Otherwise, being a leader has no genuine significance. Being a leader is not matter of value. Using your gifts where they can be of service is what is of value, regardless if they place you high or low on the world's scale of importance. *We do not address the matter of leadership in this book because leaders are more important than everyone else. We address it because leaders affect everyone else.* They either make us miserable because they are confused about their leadership gifts, or they set the rest of us free to do what we are good at doing. They either clutter the organizational landscape as drones, or they move it on to success. For that reason we ask the question:

Why do we want to be leaders?
or
Why are we leaders?

—To be important?
—To prove something?
—To show that we are better than everyone else?
—To compete?
—Because we are gifted to be?
—To serve?
—Because others expect us to be?

Leadership is for those we lead, not a stage for demonstrating our importance.

OUR COMPLEMENTS

Dependency is not usually considered to be an attribute of a leader. However, it is a basic condition of humanity. The possibility of our births was dependent upon the decisions of our parents, deliberate or otherwise. We were reared as dependents, learning languages others developed and benefiting from the efforts of others who could do what we could not. The whole fabric of civilization including education, manufacturing, agriculture, communications, and government is interdependent. The nature of organization itself is that of interdependency—of departments, divisions, functions, and employees. In his book *Management,* Peter Drucker effectively captures this in a sentence.

The purpose of an organization is to make the strengths of people productive and their weaknesses irrelevant.

By orchestrating the strengths that people bring to their work, an organization is able to do what separate individuals cannot do. To embrace the illusion that the leaders in the organization have a special calling to acquire all the gifts and become superleaders has nothing to do with reality, though it often has something to do with the values of corporate culture. This is not restricted to corporate executives, however. We find embarrassing similarities in the church, given the phenomenal number of controlling pastors we have come across over the years. They make all the decisions about everything as if they had all the gifts: financial, administrative, programmatic, personnel, educational, musical, and architectural.

Each of us needs to understand what gifts specifically complement ours. The broad view is complemented by the detail. Managers are complemented by administrators. People resources are complemented by financial resources. Sales is complemented by marketing. Leaders are complemented by supporters. Vision is complemented by feasibility, and feasibility by planning. Movers and shakers are complemented by strategists. Wherever we look we see the need for complements. The greater the degree of stewardship we apply to the interface of our gifts with those of others, the greater the quality in the results.

TEAMS

A form of complementary work relationships is seen in the team, where each person complements others to create an orchestrated approach to completing a project or running a system. Such an arrangement does not require that each participant like to function as a team member, relationally speaking. Team-player people find the relationships with other team members a stimulus to the effective application of their gifts. They are also the people who may assume that a relational team effort is the norm, and that individualistic tendencies need to be overcome. Indeed, it almost becomes a crusade for team people to do so. That tendency can polarize a team into *individualists* and *team players,* with the team people assuming that the individualists need to change. In actuality, whether one prefers to work as part of a team or to work as an individualist is an element of giftedness. Individualists are neither loners nor neurotic. They like to accomplish tasks in which one person can cover all that is required. In contrast, a team person is likely to get others involved in work, sometimes even when it easily could be done solo. Neither mode is good or bad. It is a stylistic quality in a person's interior landscape, and perceptive leaders make adjustments accordingly.

Functional Teams

The problem to solve in leading a team is one of cohesion. If the team cannot be unified entirely around team relationships, how will it hold together? The answer is found in a clearly stated common mission, with the team itself participating in the strategies of how each person interfaces with the others in terms of their respective work contributions. At that point the entire team becomes unified around the same goals, which become a script for their relationships. In this way their relationships are not artificially imposed but naturally emerge out of the work. Professionally, we have found that building a team or rebuilding a team around the team's function successfully sustains a wide diversity of participants. That is because they all have something at stake and they have all participated in the decisions that affect them. To bring this about, the leader must place the emphasis first on the mission and enable members to interface with each other based on their particular contribution. Once there is a task there is a relationship.

Vivid examples of Functional Teams can be found in the World War II movies frequently shown on cable TV. Inevitably such a movie focuses on a platoon of infantrymen or bomber crewmen who are required to train, live, and fight together. Hollywood insisted on diversity, so there are always standard stereotypes, beginning with someone from a working-class family with a Brooklyn or Philadelphia accent. He is in contrast to the wealthy member, who maintains satirical commentary about the conditions under which he has to live. There is also the braggart, the dreamer, the yokel, an ethnic person (usually Italian), and the kid who lied about his age to get into the war and who usually gets killed before the movie ends.

All of these characters are led by "Sarge," who doesn't have much schooling but is street-smart and usually has more common sense than his immediate superior. What holds all these guys together through the horrors of war? Their diversity often gets in the way of their individual relationships, but not in the way of their unity as a team. Survival unifies them as they take on the mission they have been assigned. This is a Functional Team, and it works because all their skills are exploited to advantage in order to pull off their common goal which, as a result, they always achieve. They will talk about getting back to civilian life after the war with some sorrow about breaking up their camaraderie. They all know they cannot recapture that unity in civilian life.

Unlike Sarge, in today's organization, the team leader is the one who may have the most difficulty with the process of building a Functional Team. Sarge uses common sense to get his team working together, reverting back to the informal training of playing stickball or baseball as a kid. In the organizational setting, the leader often discovers that the techniques provided in leadership development training are not realistic. They provide little for the potential clash of his or her leadership style with the operational styles of the team members. Knowing the leader's style of leadership equips us to proactively deal with that possibility. Using the Leadership Style charts, we can anticipate the degree of difficulty or the ease with which a given leader would approach this kind of team building. When working with these charts remember that there may be other gifts which may soften or firm up the conclusions, but understanding the Leadership Style is an excellent foundation for any kind of team development. It gets us thinking pragmatically about managers, who all manage in different ways and who all assume their way is the right way to manage.

LEADERSHIP REACTION TO TEAM BUILDING: EXAMPLES

STYLE	ROLE	FOCUS	RESULTS
Expert/Leader	Researcher	Information	Breakthrough

This leader would not be interested in building a team except on the basis of data that demonstrated it would be the best way to go. Probably someone else should lead the process, or if the team consists of professional peers, and it isn't too large, it could be built collaboratively.

Expert/ Leader	Maximizer	People	Improvement

This leader is not motivated to work with people relationally but is interested in people as a subject and is motivated to maximize and bring about improvement, so he or she would be favorable toward team building and have sufficient reason to lead the process.

Motivating Expert	Innovator	Concepts	Development

This leader would love this project and would want to be directly involved with the team building. However, once the team was built he or she would not have much interest in managing it.

Motivating Leader	Guide	Teams	Redirected

This is an obvious plus for building a new kind of team. Probably this person could sustain management of the team in a guidance role for a task force, but not for a long-term operation.

Manager	Director	Individuals	Goals

This leader would prefer to work with a group of professionals rather than a team and to work with individuals rather than a group. This management style is authoritative from the top down. This person would not like the team-developing process.

Managing Motivator	Persuader	Individuals and Teams	Committed

This leader would be an ideal team builder with enough managerial interests to stay for the long haul after building a highly committed team. This person could even build a team of individualist engineers.

AUTHORITY

The Focus of Authority

Leadership always involves authority. Authority is always attractive when it is *for* us. It could be your boss, it could be a police officer, it could be a government official. If the authority is on your side it always looks good. That is because the purpose of authority is to serve the people and the community. This is in contrast to leaders who believe the authority they possess is their personal right. Such arrogance is well pictured in the character of Mr. Scrooge of *A Christmas Carol* before his coerced conversion by the ghosts who were assigned to him. It is ugly. After he learns his lesson, however, our attitude toward him changes simply because his authority is now directed to the benefit of others. Leadership makes no sense whatsoever if we do not understand this. As soon as someone perceives his or her leadership role as primarily a matter of personal benefit, that person becomes corrupted.

He who is firmly seated in authority soon learns to think
security, and not progress, the highest lesson of statecraft.

J. R. Lowell

A leader is designed for the benefit of others. The role of a leader becomes an absurdity outside such service, regardless of how high on the leadership ladder one has climbed.

Since authority is a powerful tool, it might be helpful to consider two kinds of authority leaders may exercise. One is natural authority; the other, designated authority.

Natural Leadership Authority

One of the features of natural authority is that it isn't self-conscious. It emerges as an integral part of giftedness. It is exercised in such an easy way that it does not feel extraordinary to the people gifted with it. It is merely doing what is normal for them. People with this gift cannot point to how they lead, they merely do it, and it usually starts very early in life. Children who spontaneously organize games during recess, for example, begin to display a gift of some form of leadership. It will reappear repeatedly in increasingly mature ways through the years. During those times, the person's authority as a leader is enhanced by varieties of experience and education, but we have found that there will be a particular pattern to the leadership. However large the gifts, leaders with natural authority do not ascribe their abilities to techniques. They know they are leaders merely by the results.

Consistent experience with a leader who has the appropriate gifts for his or her responsibilities generates increasing trust. There are plenty of examples, perhaps beginning with our own fathers all the way back to ancient times. Alexander the Great had not only a high level of authority, but was a well-loved and respected natural leader.

Designated Authority

Designated authority is based on the power of office, rank, ownership, political clout, or combinations of these. Designated authority is borrowed authority when the occupant of the office has not done anything to merit the office, or when what he or she has done to merit the office has nothing to do with the office. There are those with designated authority who simply do not possess the gifts of leadership. Designated authority is a requirement in organizations large enough to require formal structures, and that is where the problems begin. Although any kind of authority can become preoccupied with authority *over* others rather than authority *for* others, designated authority is most prone to do so.

Experience with informal leadership demonstrates that genuine leaders act as authentic leaders without the office. In many organizations, however, it is assumed that the authority of the office will make the leader. Some will point to President Harry Truman as an example of the office making the man. The facts indicate that it would be more accurate to state that the presidential office gave power to someone who already was a leader and knew how to exercise that power for the sake of the country.

There were considerable misgivings about Truman taking the place of a presidential giant such as Franklin D. Roosevelt. It did not take long for those doubts to be expelled. Whenever designated authority is backed up by natural authority trust is established.

Trust

The complement of authority is trust. Trust is foundational to excellent leadership. It provides the security for people to concentrate on their tasks while the leader keeps an eye on the whole operation. Trust cannot be commanded. It can only be earned, and it is earned when a consistent pattern of leadership is perceived. Once earned, it can be nurtured. Here are the three great trust builders.

1. *Preserve the dignity of the individual.* This is a matter of placing a high value on persons. Highly authoritative or centralized organizations tend to engage manpower, not persons. Even aside from poor values, practically speaking, doing so ignores the connection of performance to morale. It is very costly for business to treat people as a commodity, because the resulting low morale reduces productivity. When we demean the person, we demean work, and work is what brings wealth. Aside from organizational considerations, we need to preserve the dignity of the individual merely because persons are made in the image of God. Each person's dignity is authorized by God, no matter in what kind of package a person may appear.

2. *Provide the opportunity to produce excellence by calling on the strengths the individual brings to the work.* This is a matter of job-fit. Assume each person we lead has a set of strengths to devote to work. If those capabilities *do not* fit the job, quality cannot be sustained and extra managerial time will be required to make sure the results wanted are the results produced. If those capabilities *do* fit the job, very little management time will be consumed. It doesn't take much effort to get someone to do what he or she is already motivated to do.

In some ministry, service, and parachurch organizations, there is a tendency to ignore who fits what because of the urgency of the mission. Volunteers and employees can be willingly exploited for the cause, but such exploitation has the same harvest it does anywhere else. If we claim to be doing this for God, we need to realize He does not operate under any kind of urgency, and poor stewardship of people is as questionable as the poor stewardship of money. Isn't it strange that one can be imprisoned for misusing finances, but no one questions the deliberate misuse of people? Certainly there are emergencies when everyone has to pitch in and get something done that is far removed from job-fit. Sometimes a new operation has people wearing more than one hat before things settle down. Allowances can be made, but sustained misuse of people is a poor way to carry out a worthwhile mission.

3. *Provide fitting rewards.* Aside from compensation, there are particular rewards for each person that are motivating or morale building. Ignorantly we all tend to provide rewards for others that we like for ourselves. Once we understand that each person is unique, it makes strategic sense for leaders, especially managers, to find out what rewards are appropriate for each person. Here is what one person, Robert, said to us.

"Let me begin by telling you that my boss is excellent. I love working with her, and I appreciate the opportunity to do the kind of work we are good at. But I must admit that it bugs me that when I deliver the results of any project I work on, she never says anything more than thank you."

"Well, what do you want her to say?"

"I'm not sure. I guess I want her to tell me more of what she thinks about what I've done . . . like more detail about the quality of it."

"You want a critique?"

"I guess something like that. I want to know how well she thinks the project turned out, so I can do even better next time. Obviously, I would like to hear good comments, but I wouldn't mind her pointing out something that isn't as good as it could be. That would make a big difference to me. I like to know how well I am doing."

All Robert needs at the end of any substantial project is an evaluation as to its quality. That is what we mean by a reward that makes sense to the individual. In this case, it also has the advantage of improving the quality of performance. Professionally, we would have discovered this as part of Robert's total gift inventory, but it is possible to get at this kind of information merely by asking the employee or volunteer. A little discussion would reveal what rewards are suitable, since it is a matter they probably have been agitated about from time to time. In most cases, it doesn't take much for the manager to provide it. Here are some examples of responses:

- I always work for the WOW!
- I wish I could get a grade. That's what I liked about school.
- Recognition, just some simple recognition.
- Responsibility. Give me more responsibility and show trust.
- I wouldn't mind being mentioned in a newsletter or in a staff meeting about my better accomplishments.
- Just give me a variety of assignments. I like change.
- Give me a challenging goal once in a while.
- Just say you like my work, or at least thank me.
- A reward? . . . Something that stretches me, challenges me.
- I wish they had trophies for my kind of work. I'd work hard to get one.

SELECTING AND APPRAISING PERFORMANCE

Most people tend to treat their way of operating as the norm for measuring the performance of others and so create a standard out of their own gifts. Behind the talk of appreciating diversity and the gifts of others, in the actual work situation we may judge others by the standards of our own gifts and leaders by the standards of our leadership style. That is why it is common for employers to hire people who are like themselves. In doing so, they gradually create misshapen organizations without the variety and flexibility required for vigorous organizational life. Diversity of gifts is the most precious resource an organization has, but it must be known and managed appropriately.

Today's organizations are deluded when they think they are capable of achieving even acceptable degrees of job-fit with precision. They may know how to recruit highly talented candidates by culling the best from the outstanding schools in the country, but they know little of how to effectively place, develop, and manage that talent. The splendid technical achievements of American industry have virtually no parallel in any of the people technologies. Organizational effort in that direction is not unlike an attempt to produce a Vermeer painting with a broom.

Given current standards, employees need to be careful how they respond to information given by managers using current performance appraisal procedures, even when it is a cooperative effort of both employee and manager. The conclusions may or may not be valid. It is one thing when performance is tied to production targets. If we are given the goal of producing 112 assembled widgets a week, we know clearly whether or not we reached it. If we achieve the target because we are gifted at it, all is well, especially when compensation is just. If we produce because we are persevering, but not gifted, all is not well. Job-misfit exacts a price. If we cannot produce the target because of inadequate training, management should see its error and correct it.

In all of the above, because there is measurable performance, we get clarity. Performance appraisal, however, usually has a larger objective. Such appraisal is not only a matter of critiquing work quality, but getting the big picture. It includes performance history, but also perceived attitudes and elements affecting future development of the employee. It connects what an employee has already accomplished to future development, including potential advancement. In this case, the wholesale imprecision that permeates most people development and management activities precludes most performance appraisal from being even moderately successful. When foundational assumptions are flawed, so is everything built upon them.

Both selection and performance appraisal are the responsibility of the manager who initiates them, and both processes implicate not only the employee but the leader. For example, assume the leader has made an error in selecting someone who does not fit the job and is, therefore, performing poorly. Whose fault is it? Why should the performance appraisal procedure merely critique the inadequate work of the employee without consideration of the inadequate selection procedure of the manager?

Suppose an employee does fit a project that requires creative gifts and independent decision making. Suppose further, that this person is reporting to a highly directive project manager. When performance evaluation comes up, the most common scenario would be that the employee will be faulted for lack of communication and a tendency to be independent of the project team. The employee would be confused by the impossibility of making independent decisions required by the job without being an independent person not desired by the manager. This again points out the responsibility of the leadership to either provide appropriate management for the employee or to make allowances when that is not possible. Those allowances should include a strategy for dealing with the natural clash of the manager's leadership style with the employee's inclination toward independence. No leader should attribute political or pathological motives to an employee whose gifted perfor-mance flourishes with some degree of self-direction. Productive results in any organization are enhanced far more by leaders' modifying their leadership styles than employees' modifying their ways of operating. Ob-viously, such an approach is possible where the idea of serving others through leadership is more than a formal value.

A Useful Schema

1. *Ascertain the gifts of the employee or volunteer.* When selecting a person for a position, there may be a preliminary scan of formal require-ments, such as experience, credentials, maturity, and specialized skills. However, once a candidate survives that cut, do not look at any candidate through the lens of the job. Otherwise, all you will discover is the pres-ence or absence of whatever the job requires, and that is too narrow a view of a person. Obtain as rich a portrait of the person's gifts as possible.

GIFTS

2. *Determine the requirements of the job.* This should not only in-clude WHAT is to be done, which is the focus of most job descriptions, but HOW it is to be done. For example, in any large organization the key finance person is responsible for accounting, systems, and long-range fi-nancial planning for the organization. In one organization, we found the this individual was an Expert/Leader. As such, this leader was motivated to take on long-range financial planning using analytical gifts, looking for trends, and developing pictures of the financial future. As a result, the organization was able to skirt the ups and downs of the economy. Sys-tems and accounting were covered by managers who reported to the Expert/Leader.

In replacing this leader because of retirement, knowing the WHATs would have allowed us to recommend an Expert Manager, who would have worked through two or three specialized managers in bringing about results. But because we knew not only the WHATs but the HOWs, we were clued in as well to the need for a particular kind of Managing Expert. That prevented us from damaging a company who knew that they were able to move on an even keel, but were only vaguely aware of how this was actually accomplished. We were able to explain how, over the years, everything had gradually adjusted around this financial futurist's particular gifts. At that point the company could then decide whether or not to retain this way of operating.

JOB
REQUIREMENTS

3. *The final step is to compare all you know about the person to all you know about the job.* Note that this is where it is possible to use common language. Let us look at a position in the legal department of an organization that is described in a "WHAT and HOW" statement as follows:

Research position designed to keep the Legal Department up-to-date on proposed federal legislation having the potential for making an impact upon the oil or mining industries. This is to be done by researching all designated periodicals and committee reports, plus establishing personal contacts with key legislators, committee chairpersons, and appropriate lobbyists. All research data is to be compiled and continuously updated with progress reports, in a two-page bi-weekly written report.

Given common language, a match might look like this:

WHAT THE JOB REQUIRES	WHAT THE PERSON HAS
Researching	Researching
Interviewing	Conferring*
Information Gathering	Information Gathering
Reducing Data	Data Gathering*
Reading	Reading
Writing	Writing
Organizing	Structuring*
Establishing Relationships	Facilitating
Updating	•
Communicating	Communicating
	Developing Systems**
	Mediating Conflicts**

This comparison illustrates quite a good match between the person and the job. One item is missing (•), three items are not exact but close (*), and two items are present but not needed in the job (**).

When the language we use to describe the job is exactly the same language we use to describe the person, we can precisely compare the degree of job-fit. We can do this because we are comparing specifics, not interpreting generalities. For example, if we were to identify the candidate as an inductive reasoner or a brilliant student, we would be speaking in terms that may be true but are inappropriate to job-match. In the columns above, either the candidate does or does not have the capabilities of reducing data, or establishing relationships, or writing, or researching. The data needed to ascertain job-fit or leadership styles is too specific to be covered by personality types, such as introvert, or temperament types, such as sanguine or phlegmatic. Using such typology is like informing us that the pillar we are choosing to hold up the roof is yellow instead of telling us the weight it can bear.

When we overlay the strengths a person brings to the work to the requirements of the job we will end up with the degree of job-fit (represented by c in the circle graphic below). No job-fit we know reaches perfect congruence, so we will observe a surplus of gifts that will not be called on by the job (a in the circle graphic below). Most of us will attempt to reshape our jobs to include the use of these surplus gifts without regard for whether the organizational mission or the job description requires them.

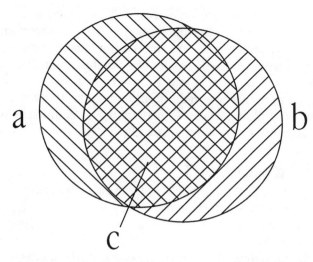

The presence of these surplus gifts—represented in the example we are using by the items *Developing Systems* and *Mediating Conflicts* —can be affirmed as a resource to be used when the opportunity calls for it. Meanwhile, encouragement should be given to apply these gifts in volunteer work, or service to others, or in leisure activities.

We observe that the job requirements in the example are not entirely covered, in that *Updating* is missing (*b* in the circle graphic). What the employee brings to the job does not cover this portion of the job requirements. Given the high degree of job-fit, this candidate has good reason to cover this responsibility by exercising self-discipline. Good job-fit generates the energy to do so. In this case, however, *Updating* as a job element does not stand as an independent activity. It is built into the process of preparing the report, so it will create no problem. Otherwise, training an employee to better cover job responsibilities for which he does not have the relevant gifts can be helpful. It should be assumed that skills acquired in this way will drop away when they are no longer needed.

Looking at Performance

With the above understanding of job-fit, we do not recommend combining *c* (job-fit) and *b* (job-misfit) in evaluating job success. Doing that invariably means praising the large fit and condemning the small misfit. It ends up being one of those "We-appreciate-the-great-job-you-are-doing-but . . ." statements. Those "buts" will contaminate the otherwise valuable data accumulating in the employee's file. The file should contain the gold—the history of the individual's giftedness applied to the job. That history becomes the data that can guide the organization in using the employee wisely.

Does this mean we ignore *b?* No. It is evaluated in terms of how well the employee has handled the limitation. That information, however, is kept separate from the gold. In some ways it becomes an evaluation of the employee's ability to be disciplined in handling the misfit elements of the job. Of course, as soon as such elements can be covered by those who are gifted to do them, a trade should be made. That can be done for everyone when building a complementary team. As much as is possible, the misfit elements are traded to those gifted to do them.

DOING WHAT WE OUGHT

Everybody suffers the myopia of their gifts. Obviously, all of us see things our way, which is too narrow a way to enable us to understand every situation. Therefore, if a leader at the top of an organization only makes decisions from his or her perspective, a percentage of those decisions will be out of line. Remember, no one has all the gifts.

To know one's own gifts is to know what we want to do and how we want to do it. Developmental people are always thinking developmentally about almost everything. Strategic people are continually strategizing every opportunity they get. Maximizers are always thinking of how to get more out of less. They do it at work, they do it at home, and they will do it for you, too, if you let them.

These are our gifts, not static skills. They prompt us to move. They push us into action, and we want and intend to do something very specific.

Once we can perceive our *wants* in this regard, we can entertain another possibility, and that is the *ought*. This writer is highly developmental, and in my business I am ready to run with every developmental opportunity that presents itself. However, that is not always best for the business. Some developmental projects should be put off for another time. Others are not appropriate for the business. So, what I need to do every time I look at possibilities, is to ask a simple question, but one that is critical to success: *I know what I want to do, but in view of the needs of the business, what ought I do?* Asking such a question makes no bones about what I naturally want. I do not need to deny my interest or my passion to do what I personally would prefer to do. But the sheer logic of what I ought to do quickly stifles the possibility of taking on projects inappropriate for the business, or projects that should be shelved for a while. Frequently, I do not have the appropriate gifts to make this decision by myself. That means I bring in the people who can complement my perspective with theirs. Our objective knowledge of each other's gifts gives us great freedom to decide together what we ought to do. Sometimes one person has the best insight, sometimes another. It makes no difference as long as we make good decisions.

> *Where no counsel is, the people fall: but in the multitude of counselors, there is safety.*
>
> Proverbs 11:14 KJV

DECISION MAKING

Human beings are characterized by the mysterious presence of will-power. We conduct our lives by continually making decisions for ourselves and for others. We are not propelled by instinct. We make most of our moves by choice. The fabric of our lives is woven from thousands upon thousands of decisions, good and bad, made by individuals on all levels.

All of this becomes even more dramatic when applied to leaders. It is anyone's prerogative to make a bad decision for his private life, but when a decision is made by a leader, it can poison the operation of which he or she is in charge. Too often, a bad decision by a highly placed leader is bad for thousands, and in the case of leaders in government, for millions of citizens. Whenever we notice dejection in an organization it is usually traced to someone, somewhere, making bad choices. This simple fact stimulates our belief in the need to understand and manage the decision-making processes within any organization. That includes tracking the result of any decision to discover the best ways for a particular organization to make productive decisions.

There are times when we are appalled at the arrogance with which leaders assume their decisions should receive unquestioned acceptance, merely on the basis of who made them. The confidence leaders can place in their own decision-making abilities is astounding when viewed from the outside. Embarrassingly, had we the ability to see into a leader's mind, we probably would find his or her degree of confidence very much like our own. Many of us think we are close to infallible. It is similar to what happens at every meeting any of us attends. All the participants say to themselves, *Well, there may be those who are smarter than I am, but I really know what is going on.* Curiously, we do that while knowing that if we were to interview every participant to discover what actually took place in the meeting, we would find widely varying descriptions. The degree of focus we give to any agenda item is idiosyncratic. There is no norm for any of it.

Because we live in a rationalistic age, there is a tendency to assume that there is a normative process for making decisions. Yet, in reality, all decisions are similar only in that they end with a choice or a judgment, and the process by which conclusions are achieved differs with each person. There is no one right way of making a decision; rather, there is for each of us our particular style in deciding. Each of us is effective in making certain kinds of decisions and ineffective elsewhere. Some people can work their way through all kinds of subtle people-behaviors and are virtually incompetent in making a business decision. One individual thinks intuitively, another logically. This person is triggered into a decision-making mode by crises or emergencies or problems, another by the ongoing need to keep the operation on track. What freezes one person, releases another.

Decision Categories

For purposes of clarity, we organize decisions into three categories.

1. *Circumstantial decisions*. These are decisions that are driven by the immediacy of the situation. There is very little process and much reaction or response. Hunger forces a decision to eat. A child running onto the road causes us to swerve the car. An emergency causes us to help. The dog barks for the door to be opened. A bill has to be paid. We simply do what we need to do. We don't have to think much about these.

2. *Developmental decisions*. These decisions are a response to information that comes to us from others and affects us personally. We call them developmental because they usually cause us to understand something we otherwise would not have examined, or to experience something we would not have thought about on our own, or to act in a way that is foreign to our pattern of operating. Someone gets us to think about what we would not have thought about on our own. Someone else gets us to consider opportunities we otherwise would not have seen or understood.

These opportunities come about because we are social beings. As such, we are responsible for one another and naturally try to influence each other. All of this is a product of family, community, and friendship. A teacher encourages a student to go to college when the student comes from a family that doesn't encourage the girls to go beyond high school. A friend introduces us to a book or a movie that opens another world to us. Someone close to us challenges us about our lifestyle.

Probably the most vivid example of this is in the story of the apostle Paul's conversion. He was on the road to Damascus and was invaded by unavoidable truth. He changed radically and thereby changed the world. He had not intended to do that, but he encountered information for which there was only one response that made any sense. In the apostle Paul, the grace of the invasion came from God. More often, this kind of grace comes to us through friends and mentors. We are unaware of our self-centeredness, and someone lets us know our attitude. We are too narrow in our thinking, and a friend points out possibilities we never would have considered. The decisions we make in these settings can be life changing. They always depend upon others, sometimes driven by enthusiasm, other times by anger or frustration, sometimes by love.

Leaders often become isolated and thereby cut themselves off from the grace of being challenged or advised by others. Allowing people into our lives to relate, question, and discuss is how most of us discover areas that we should address that would not have otherwise occurred to us. It is the best corrective we know to lopsided leadership. Be sure that when we are lopsided leaders, we never know our condition. That is why we must make it easy for others to advise us. The flatter the organizational structure, the easier it is for that to take place; the more hierarchical, the less it happens.

3. *Motivated decisions.* There are certain opportunities for making decisions to which we are naturally drawn because they relate to what we like to do. In fact, our interest can be so focused that we barely know that we are making decisions while we make them. If we examine those times carefully (and they are different from person to person), we will discover that there is a consistent pattern to the way we make decisions. This pattern is part of how we are gifted to operate.

Brendan, for example, has discovered that he is most satisfied with work that allows him to perfect something. He loved making model airplanes as a boy, and as an adult he will occasionally take on a model ship project—which he finishes in exquisite detail. Another project, which engages countless hours, is the restoration of a sports car with innumerable coats of meticulously applied paint, polished to a gleaming finish. Whether he works on a model or on a car, Brendan is fascinated with precision work, where he goes over the details until he achieves perfection. Brendan makes decisions the same way. He will go over the details of the available data repeatedly so he can make a decision that is flawless. That can become a problem, because he finds himself procrastinating the final decision in order to assure himself that there is no mistake. Once the decision is made, he will review it again, wondering if it is absolutely correct. This looks like extreme behavior to his friends, but in actuality it is normal for Brendan.

In dealing with decisions of small importance, Brendan needs to appreciate why others are impatient with his deliberations. He should avoid making a principle out of his style ("A person ought always to be careful when he makes decisions"). He will do a masterful job with decisions requiring a review of quantities of information. Where someone else might miss an important piece of data, Brendan will have all the bases covered. Anyone seeing him in the latter mode of decision making would have a vastly different opinion about his decisiveness compared to what happens when he strains the patience of waitresses and friends while he mulls over a menu.

Carol is gifted as a leader. She is gifted to be in control and to take command of situations requiring considerable organizing, especially if it is written or graphic data. She naturally wants to determine how things will be categorized, so she makes decisions quite easily. This is in contrast to her brother John, who is likely to be a bit more thoughtful about how he makes decisions because he is gifted with strong evaluating abilities, especially where there are subtleties of style to be discerned. This fits his career, which involves documenting and authenticating works of art. Once he has come to a conclusion his decisions are rarely challenged. However, John has to exercise discipline in order to conquer the sloth that seems to encompass him when he has to deal with financial matters.

Context

Making good decisions professionally does not guarantee good decision making everywhere. Decisive leaders at work do not necessarily make decisive leaders at home. Some people make amazingly creative decisions but are poor at those involved in running a home or an office. There are individuals who swiftly decide under the same pressure that immobilizes others.

Subject

Decisions are affected by subject matter. For example, people who like to work with intangibles do better with ethical questions than would the bottom-line decision makers. Highly conceptual thinkers may analyze complex abstract data and emerge with clear decisions, whereas simple pragmatic situations confuse them.

Assessing Capability

In describing the above people, we are just considering a few factors to provide an idea of how our gifts are going to affect our decision making in spite of what others may or may not prefer. As we become aware of how we have operated in making decisions in the past we have a key to how we make decisions now. As we enrich our understanding, we can anticipate where direct involvement in a decision would be wise and where we should engage others in the process.

The questions presented below are provided to sensitize us to the way we operate when required to make a decision, and to consider how we might enhance our effectiveness.

1. *Objective.* Is the reason for making this decision clear to me? Do I understand what I am after and why? If there is a problem, do I know exactly what it is? Or am I like the person who is deciding which software program to use without understanding why the software is needed?

2. *Focus.* What kind of information do I need to make a decision? How much information do I need, considering the nature of the decision? Am I like the person who is curious about anything to do with the subject of marketing but not considering how to apply this knowledge?

3. *Sources.* Considering who I am, what is the best way for me to get information? Talk with experts? Interview the key players? Use reference libraries? Go to where the research is being done? In this case, is it best to get information the way I naturally am inclined to get it, or would it be better to pursue the facts another way?

4. *Process.* How is it best for me to process the information I have gathered? Read it over and take notes? Discuss it with friends? Confer with an expert? Get somebody to hold me accountable to process it?

5. *Thinking.* Does this decision require me to work at the data carefully and logically like a math problem, or do I have to make an intuitive leap? Does the process I want to apply to this situation take time, or does it tend to be swift? Is that bad or good in this case? If it is bad for this decision-making process, what should be done to correct that? Who or what can help me come to the best conclusion?

6. *Action.* Once the decision is made, is there an action that needs to be taken? Am I motivated to take such action? Are there any obstacles to my taking action? If so, considering how I operate, what is the best prescription I can put in place to help me?

CHAPTER 10

HOW SHALL WE
THEN BEHAVE?

CHARACTER

The continuing and most serious misfortune all organizations face is the lust leaders maintain for their position as leaders. They become a class unto themselves, with the first claim in their lives being their position and their power. This is true no less in the church than in the corporation, and no less in government than in universities.

In Business

This disease cripples business everywhere. At the time of this writing we know of a well-known, multi-national corporation that is stagnating because immobilized leaders won't make a place for fresh leadership to bring vision and energy to the tremendous resources of which that corporation is supposed to be a steward. They are now running on the profitable momentum of the past, but without energy for a profitable thrust into the future. The board of directors is essentially made up of people willing to say yes to the status quo. On the surface, all looks well, but this corporation is dying. When it does die, the leaders will escape with grand financial packages.

In Churches

We also know of churches who have pastors who assume that their preoccupation with their authority and position is itself the voice of their calling. They mistake the call of their ambition for the call of God. Their first allegiance is to their ideas and their plans, and they refer to God in packaging their intentions. They appear to be excellent leaders able to stir up their congregations to move ahead and accomplish useful ministry, but they are the sole source of power, and they intend to remain so. No theological gloss or ecclesiastical success will change that fact. In these churches, the only leaders who gain positions under the pastor are those who can be controlled by the pastor. Selection of these leaders appears to be a spiritual process, but is in actuality an arbitrary political decision.

In Government

We all know of representatives for whom we voted to make a difference in Washington, D.C., who, once they were in the circles of power, replaced their well-intentioned crusades with the lifestyle of the ambitious. The necessary agenda was abandoned for practical self-interest.

One characterization of an ideal civilization would be the ability to move its leaders around with great flexibility so that the right person, with the appropriate gifts, would be in precisely that place where he or she could produce exactly what is needed. That is exactly what we do not get, nor do we realistically expect. The dominant reason is that leaders on every level from supervisor to president cling to their positions, importance, and power.

For the reason behind this state of affairs, we refer you again to the story of Eden. In doing so, we realize that as we point out this characteristic sin of leadership, we cannot do so from the position of innocence. We have sinned in this area ourselves. Nevertheless, no matter the degree of our personal failures, that does not mean that the gravity of the problem across the society as a whole should be ignored. The larger the organization, the more serious the situation, not only because of the massive effect upon thousands of people, but because of the greater difficulty in addressing it. It is one thing to change directions when riding a pony, another to redirect a rhinoceros.

The problem is essentially an issue of character. The antidote for the disease is for the community to place high value on personal character development. Historically, that has only happened when a passion for integrity is driven by convictions of substance. Otherwise, we end up with mere academic training in theoretical ethics, which is too mild a medicine to counteract the fierceness of inordinate ambitions.

This is the insurmountable problem of the secular world. How does a secular society get people to do what is right, if the reason for doing it is merely legal? In the United States, the difficult but real pluralism of the past is being seriously challenged. The secularists intend to excise the Judeo-Christian passion behind morality in which God is the ultimate judge, leaving behind a merely antiseptic pragmatic rationalism as the fuel for right behavior. Intellectual history does not encourage their success. It takes more than that to curtail the power seeker. Organizations will eventually die and be replaced by new ones. That is why it is crucial to repeatedly engage the subject of character in any consideration of leadership success. That is also why it is important to appreciate the synagogues and churches present in our communities, as they remind us of the kind of character God's justice demands.

The secular world often assumes that the people who gather in churches perceive themselves to be the good people. They have it reversed. We can understand why. Though the church is really composed of people who realize they are sinners who have experienced God's grace, sometimes Christians forget that. So we need here to reaffirm a truth basic to Christianity. Character development is not a matter of doing good deeds to establish a relationship with God. It has to do with who we are because of what God has done for us. It has to do with the quality of who we are, the quality of our lives. If we are leaders, it also includes the character and meaning of leadership in view of who God has made us to be.

THE RULES

Most discussions about character seem focused upon coercing behavior others require of us. That began, for most of us, with our parents and teachers. It continues today with devotional books and sermons insisting repeatedly that we never hit the target exactly right. We are told to try harder and then even harder. It all adds up to a nonstop expectation for continual improvement.

In such an approach to behavior, the emphasis is almost always upon the rules. That, as a matter of course, becomes irritating, because the rules are never satisfied. The classic expression of this dissatisfaction is found in the words of the apostle Paul.

I do not understand my own actions. For I do not do what I want,
but I do the very thing I hate. Now if I do what I do not want, I agree
that the law is good. So then it is no longer I that do it, but sin which
dwells within in me. *(Romans 7:15–17 RSV)*

Many of us can identify with the frustration expressed by Paul as he
describes the confusion of mixed motives in his life. We often look at the
contradictions in our lives and wonder how to make sense of them. But if
our focus is solely on the rules, we will never make sense of them. Rules
have no heart, no mercy, no forgiveness, no message but that we have
failed. Sensitivity to this has much to do with the temper of our leadership, because we often are required to be the authority behind some of
the rules. That causes pain for many leaders, who are required to judge
rule breakers when they are themselves rule breakers in some area of
living. That is an unavoidable condition of being human, a condition that
should encourage mercy and humility in every leader. It is a strange tension, but one brilliantly portrayed in a letter by the apostle John.

God is light; in him there is no darkness at all. If we claim to have
fellowship with him yet walk in the darkness, we lie and do not live
by the truth. But if we walk in the light, as he is in the light, we have
fellowship with one another, and the blood of Jesus, his Son,
purifies us from all sin. If we claim to be without sin, we deceive
ourselves and the truth is not in us. If we confess our sins, he is
faithful and just and will forgive our sins and purify us from all
unrighteousness. . . . I write this to you so that you will not sin. But if
anybody does sin, we have one who speaks to the Father in our
defense—Jesus Christ, the Righteous One. *(1 John 1:5–2:1 NIV)*

Since character is not a matter of rules, what is it? Character has to
do with the distinctive qualities of the person God intended us to be
when He made us, so that our actions both moral and functional express
what He created us to be. However, He does not force us to become
persons of character. We are not puppets. He gives us power to choose to
become persons of character. That choice opens the way for Him to act
on our behalf. He sets our real selves free. Our character, then, is not
something we *have*. It is someone we *are*. That being so, mere obedience
to the law, that is, making ourselves behave by sheer discipline, is not the
goal God has for us. Recognition of the rules enables us to know what
good character should look like, but it is impotent in transforming us into
that person. Therefore, once the broken rules reveal our condition, God
entices us into a relationship with Him. The effect of this intimacy is that
we become increasingly who we should be. This does not happen from

the outside in, the way rules operate. It works from the inside out, the way God operates.

So that we are able to meet the Law's requirements, so long
as we are living no longer by the dictates of our sinful
nature, but in obedience to the promptings of the Spirit.
                                                        Romans 8:4 PHILLIPS

That emphasizes the quality of the person, not the accounting of the rules. That is why we define character as the spiritual shape of an individual. It opens the way to see the substance and the beauty of who God is sculpting us to be in our inner nature, as we do what He has gifted us to do. God has His eyes not only upon what we are now doing, but upon who we are increasingly becoming for eternity. With that perspective, we can abandon the arid legalities of satisfying the rules to pursue the pleasure of delighting the great Sculptor.

CHARACTER AND OUR GIFTS

If we insist on retaining a merely legal view of character, it is difficult to imagine any delight that God might have in it beyond that of order. We expect He gets no more pleasure over such human obedience than that derived from an acorn obeying the law of falling down to the ground rather than up and away from it. For God, the direction acorns fall is not relevant except for the matter of getting acorns to the ground. So God insists that acorns will fall downward. That is where they belong so they can root and eventually become the lofty, arboreal giants God intended them to be. With that grand view of an acorn's future, how should God respond to a convocation of acorns gathered to protest the requirement that they fall down? With what attitude should God listen to their petition for greater freedom to fall in any direction they prefer?

Let us go further. Imagine the ludicrous scene of an acorn stubbornly refusing to germinate because it has ambitions of eventually bearing apples rather than more acorns. The deluded acorn has no capability of becoming anything other than it was made to be and, in fact, *has no capacity to gain pleasure as anything else.* The acorn had better take root as what it is. If not, if it refuses its calling, it rejects life. There is no other package in which life can be received than that in which it already appears for the acorn, and also for you and for me.

To be a leader in God's scheme of things is to be a particular leader and not any other. Our freedom to be ourselves resides in the limitation that we can be no other. For our own sake, we must resist the temptation to grasp a position that does not fit us. This is true whether career ambitions drive us to higher misfit roles or spiritual ambitions reduce us to false humility. Given permission, God will crush a lust to go higher or to go lower, in the same way He kills any illusion. Seeing people choose to become who He created them to be is His great delight. What we have to learn again and again is that it is also the only possible delight for us.

Here are three simple principles to guide us in this process.

1. *Accept who we are.* We come into the meaning of our individual lives when we take who we are already, our time, our place, and our gifts with gratitude. God's eye is upon what we do with what He has given, not upon the world's estimate of our importance. We do not have the remotest idea of who is really important or who is genuinely the most beautiful. In the current scheme of things, we may be highly placed or become famous. That is only of importance to the degree it fits our calling and character.

> *I bid every one among you not to think of himself more highly than he ought to think, but to think with sober judgment, each according to the measure of faith which God has assigned him.*
>
> —Romans 12:3 KJV

2. *Express who we are.* As we work through the smog of ignorance we have about ourselves and discover the gifts God has given, both natural and spiritual, we are to express who we are in our work and our relationships. God takes pleasure in all the plumbers, masons, homemakers, managers, accountants, artists, economists, poets, teachers, basket weavers, farmers, builders, lawyers, mathematicians, programmers, physicians, engineers, pastors, students, baseball players, psychologists, astronomers, singers, and writers who are expressing gifts that fit their work. He takes no pleasure in those who for the sake of prestige, power, fame, or greed take on work that does not fit their gifts.

As we say this, however, we also must recognize the difficult situations. God is pleased with those who take up work fitted for their gifts. But His eye is also upon the sacrifice of those who are called to work that economic or social conditions or personal situations prevent. At least, when such people know their gifts, they know the nature of the sacrifice and why the pain. If they know God, they can bear it, because He experienced infinitely worse. More than that, the great Sculptor makes astounding beauty out of sacrifice. My father went through the Great Depression. Responsible for his family, he was not in a position to take a job that fit him. He was living during a time when merely a job was a blessing. He was faithful to his responsibilities as a provider, even though it was a sacrifice. Only as I have come to know what we have discovered about the profound nature of human giftedness, have I realized the depth of his sacrifice.

3. *Do what is appropriate to do.* Since God has a sensitive relationship with each of us, He always responds to our uniqueness. Each person's relationship with Him is unlike any other. Each of us can know an aspect of God's nature that is hidden from others. Since this is no longer a legal matter of keeping the rules, but of becoming the unique character God intended in creating each of us, His presence in us can direct us to do what we ought to do in any situation. These "oughts" differ for everybody. They differ in terms of integrity, timing, role, and goals.

Integrity

We are all to be honest, but we will express this honesty in different ways in different contexts and with different results. The intensity of honesty in matters of finance are far different for the accountant than for the poet. The degree of honesty of expression is different for the journalist than for the engineer. We are all to be humble, but what this means in one life is different from what it means in another. Billy Graham obviously has gifts that enable him to gain the attention of millions of people. Gaining attention is a gift that God has given him. He had no choice about the matter. What he does with the gift is something else. It could be used to become a star, or for service.

Humility in Graham would not be denying his gift and abandoning the millions of seekers God attracts to the gospel through him. That would be a lie. If Graham assumed that he was clever enough to have attained his gifts, rather than being a steward of what God had given, he would have a character flaw with which to deal. After all, is there anything in us or about us that does not come from God? Are we the inventors of the gifts? Are we the originators of the energy that makes them function? When we understand the correct answers to these questions and act like it, we will have acquired some fragments of humility. Humility is the condition of those who apprehend reality. The reality here is that all gifts come from God.

Timing

Sensitivity to timing is an inherent ingredient in spiritual maturity. Jesus was born in the fullness of time and was sensitive to the unfolding of the times. "My time has not come," He would say, or, "The time is at hand." All His acts were the intersections of His will and right timing. Not surprisingly, we do not always know the right time to use our gifts. In fact, it is often worse than that. We may be so compulsive that we think all the time is the right time for our gifts. That childish assumption is present in too many of us.

All of us need to be sensitive as to when we ought to exercise our gifts and when we should withhold them. In the case of leaders, this is of major importance because, as we repeatedly state, others, sometimes many others, are affected. Untimely decisions in any kind of organization ultimately affect the well-being of the whole community. That is why receiving counsel from people with differing gifts is not only advisable but often critical to determine what should happen.

Prayer, too, is requisite for becoming sensitive to timing. It is an activity that by nature requires quieting the mind to receive from God. That is the state in which we need to be as we look away from what we intend, to what God is orchestrating. We should want not only to do the right thing, but to do it at the right time so our decisions as leaders can be of value in the whole panorama of what God is accomplishing.

Role

As the timely move is being made, the question to ask is, "What role should I take?" We have different nuances to our gifts. Wisdom urges a strategic decision based on what role we *ought* to take rather than the role we *want* to take. Always look at what is required by the situation and become strategic about the roles to be played. The drama director conducts auditions based on the script. The script determines who should do what. So it is with any organization. Many good plans have been ruined by leaders who had the power to insert themselves into inappropriate roles in order to get the credit for what would have otherwise brought about superlative results.

Goals

We tend to assume that leaders determine goals as a result of a logical process. That underestimates how unique people are. We not only differ from each other in how we process information, but our motivational bent can prevent us from arriving at the appropriate conclusions. Yes, it is true that sometimes we may not have adequate information, and sometimes our analysis is wrong. But very often we suffer from the bias imposed by our own gifts.

- We know of a company that has made a decision to retrench. All the information they have compiled clearly supports that decision. However, they have just acquired a president who is a Motivating Visionary. How do you think he will view a plan for retrenchment? What kind of scenarios might develop, given his gifts?

- The board of directors of a foundation has decided that its key managers should be empowered to share more in top-level strategy decisions. The foundation is managed by an individual whose leadership style is that of a Controlling Director. What interest would he have in empowering his key managers? What might be some of the problems?

We can assume that that president and that director will look at their respective situations in very different ways. An uncritical faith in their own opinions could eventually cripple their respective organizations. An awareness of their own limitations might be the saving factor for each organization. We repeat: no one has all the gifts. No one sees the entire picture. No one has total understanding but God Himself.

We should not be surprised that a pastor who is a Motivating, Recruiting leader would overemphasize evangelism. It should be no shock that a Maintaining, Manager who is president of an ailing business calls a halt to precisely the innovative efforts that would assure the company's future. But both leaders are ignoring a fundamental rule: Do not make a principle out of gifted inclinations. Here are several examples of leaders announcing principles with the assumption that they will work for everyone.

Directive Manager to Creative Developer:

PRINCIPLE: "If you don't know precisely where you are going, you don't know what you are doing."

FACT: This manager, who always sets goals, does not understand that for a Creative Developer playing with ideas precedes action, and a dozen failed experiments generates a discovery. Creativity functions at the developmental edge where the next step cannot be seen, where nothing exists. How can someone know where he or she is going in such a landscape? Creative people intuitively move ahead with nothing but the broadest goals, and because of the peculiar nature of their gifts, they arrive. Once they arrive they see where they intended to go. Now they know the goal toward which they were moving, but could not know before they began.

Technical Manager to business students:

PRINCIPLE: "All great leaders are first and foremost excellent strategists."

FACT: There are all kinds of leaders, and only some of them are strategic in their way of approaching goals. Very often Visionary Leaders require others to translate their foresight and passion into a mission statement, and from there to a strategic plan before anything actually happens.

Manager to staff:

PRINCIPLE: "We need to do more things to stimulate innovation. Free yourselves up. Reorganize again and again. Try different combinations in order to shake the place up."

FACT: Innovation cannot be stimulated in people with zany stimuli. Coming up with novel or bizarre combinations is neither innovation nor creativity. Periodic shake-ups may be a good antidote to ossification, but for the most part, one cannot stimulate creativity or innovation in people unless it already is present. If an innovative team is required, select innovative people.

JUDGMENT

How secure many of us feel about our own wisdom, and how secure we are in our own perceptions. There is a part of us that judges everything and everyone around us with great confidence, as if our intellects were somehow spared the curse of the Fall. We should, and sometimes do, know better. So even while we celebrate the wealth of giftedness in people, we should never underestimate how those same gifts can turn us into narrow-minded persons. Because of the limitation of our gifts, there are some things we never think about. Yet, on occasion, those are the very things that are critical. We respect the gifts of leaders, but realize those gifts do not protect us from mistakes, sometimes severe ones. For that reason, those of us who are Christian leaders must take advantage of a devotional life in which we can hear God's guidance and learn to accept the limitations of our gifts. Such acceptance will encourage us to tap other gifts in order to gain a richer perspective. We might then appreciate the beauty of an organization, be it a committee or corporation, performing with all the players in the right place, including the leader.

SECTION FOUR

———◦◦◦◦◦———

THE ORGANIZATION

The whole is more than the sum of its parts.

CHAPTER 11

————⌒◎⌒————

ORGANIZATIONS

One of the recurring fantasies we hear from people whose lives have been overly fragmented by their careers is the idea of buying a small farm somewhere and getting back to the land. This is quite the reverse of our agrarian past, when the fantasy was to leave the farm and do something exciting in the city. It illustrates the contrast between the period when most employment was sustained by small farms, and today, when most employment is by institutions.

On the farm, job satisfaction depended upon only a few factors, such as pay, the hours one worked, and how one was treated by the boss. In modern organizations, we still have the same basic set of factors, but added to them are the complexities of modern institutions. We end up not only concerned that our individual careers flourish, but that the organizations for which we work also do well. The degree to which individuals succeed is inextricably tied to the success of institutions; no one survives if institutions do not. This symbiosis is so critical that a discussion of leadership requires consideration of the nature of organizations in which leadership is enacted.

A survey of all the problems with which organizations contend leads us to a simplistic conclusion. The problem with most organizations is that they do not understand organizations. This summation is stated with the realization that no organization can be fully understood, not only because organizations are complex, but also because they are always changing. That ever-changing complexity presents people with any number of choices in how they can define an organization. What is needed is a basic perspective that not only leads to understanding a particular institution, but makes as large a pragmatic difference as possible. The following has been helpful in enabling us to swiftly get to the core of organizational issues, regardless of the kind of institution or its focus.

BASIC PERSPECTIVE

Organizations exist because people are, by nature, dependent. People cannot survive by themselves, so they cooperate. The more people there are, and the more they cooperate, the greater the necessity for organization. The more complex and specialized the organization, the greater the necessity for institutionalization. All institutions are developed by people, for people, and are composed of people.

There is a facile conclusion that can be derived from this. If we want to grasp the essence of what an organization is, we must first think of it in terms of *people*. That will not only enrich the way we think, it will lead to more practical conclusions about organizations than if we define them in any other terms. This view contrasts with the many narrower definitions that picture organizations primarily as entities that are legal, or functional, or administrative, or physical, or hierarchical, or political. Those are all legitimate and more commonly used categories than the one we are identifying as critical, but they are all too narrow.

Whether we concentrate on a part of, or the whole organization, the more an organization understands people, what they bring to the organization, and their functional relationships, the more effective it can become. All legal efforts, management, business processes, and sales ventures operate best when people are the dominant consideration of the organization. We emphasize that this does not mean recognizing people as one component among others, such as administration, business, or management. It means *perceiving all the roles and functions of an organization through the lens of people as the primary category.*

In looking at business organizations, for example, if we understand people first, then we can understand management, because management means people getting people to do work. Understand people first, and we can understand sales, because sales involves people getting people to come to decisions. Understand people first, and we can understand manufacturing, because it is people who will design the product and run the machines that produce it. The same can be said for schools in relation to the learning process, and to churches in regard to evangelism and counseling, and to families in relation to parenting and nurturing the people who will do it all. The life of any organization appears far richer when perceived through the lens of unique people with specific gifts, rather than through any other category. Here are two examples to illustrate this, one from business, the other from church.

Business Example: Recruiting Salespeople

In the business setting, recruiters are constantly looking for salespeople. They identify as potential candidates those who "have a certain gleam in their eyes." Such candidates appear to like people and easily make an impact upon them, so recruiters want to hire them for sales. From our perspective of giftedness, however, we find that often something else is going on that recruiters miss. Some of these potential candidates are motivated to persuade, and they will move steadily toward closing a sale. There are others who also want to make an impact upon people, but only to establish a personal relationship. They have no interest in moving anyone toward a sales closing because they might get a no, and that is an intolerable possibility for them. That makes the wrong impact and ends the relationship. So if success for a company requires closing the sale by asking for a signature on a contract, this is not the kind of person to hire for sales. Hiring should be based on the actual gifts candidates possess. Recruiters need to use greater precision when looking at candidates.

Once aboard, the new salesperson will go through sales training, much of which will be devoted to getting the salesperson to conform to a particular script. This script usually systematizes the sales techniques of one outstanding salesperson, perhaps the trainer or the sales manager. It is assumed that if everyone imitates these techniques, sales must inevitably follow. That fallacy would be cleared up if companies took seriously the matter of individual uniqueness. The way someone sells or persuades depends on the nature of his or her gifts. One person persuades through strategies, another through needs, some through relationships, others through expertise. That is why people who are gifted at sales fit certain products or services better than others. Some can easily sell a concept, whereas others must have a concrete product. Providing sales training that equips salespeople to sell in terms of their gifts imparts authority to sales presentations that otherwise would be absent. Certainly there are qualities about a product that require standardized elements in the sales presentation, but the energy of quality sales resides in the gifts of the presenter.

In summary, selection of salespesons should be based on whether the way the individual sells fits the product or service to be sold. Training and sales management should be based on tapping what the salesperson is motivated to deliver, not upon the imposition of a standardized model. That is how looking through the lens of people rather than sales techniques enhances business in a fundamental manner.

Example from the Churches: Church Growth

Church leaders often duplicate the mistakes of the corporation. This is seen in church growth programs. Most of the programs are based on studies of particular churches that have demonstrated strong growth and transferring the conclusions of those studies to other churches. The procedure is based on two fallacies. The first is the belief that the program itself brought about the growth in the originating church. Anytime we have observed genuine church growth (new converts), it was because of specific people who exercised the appropriate gifts. God works through the gifts of His people. Sometimes those gifts can be found in a developmental pastor or in an evangelist who knows to connect converts to mentors and teachers. Other times they emerge out of a group of believers who orchestrate ways to attract and develop new people. Sustained expansion was always through the specific gifts of particular people. That was true of growth in churches that did not seem to be inspired by any special visitation of God. It was also true where a deep spiritual renaissance was being initiated by God, sometimes to the surprise of the leaders.

The second fallacy is the belief that a program is automatically transferable to any other situation. A church must look at its own community, its resources, its unique relationship with God, and the kinds of gifts God has provided in the congregation before deciding what it should do in *any* matter. There is nothing wrong with programs as long as they are suitable and are understood to be tools. God brings about genuine church growth, and He does not always do it immediately in terms of numbers. His church is always growing, but not in any manner similar to the patterns and process of business. It is not a matter of sales and marketing; it is a matter of the Holy Spirit's convicting, converting, and nurturing. God cannot and will not be managed. That is why so many impatient churches settle for sales and marketing. We do not denigrate research and program development. There is much to be learned about how to make a difference to society around us, how to communicate, and how to develop churches. We need those who are gifted in teaching us. But we must be careful about our basic assumptions.

UNIQUENESS

Organizations need to know who they are to be effective. Since every organization is composed of different people with differing gifts, attempting to attain particular goals, every organization must be unique. Knowledge of this uniqueness can be a guide toward clarifying the appropriate niche the organization should occupy in the marketplace or community to be successful.

Without reflecting upon its own uniqueness, an organization may end up searching for organizational models to fill the void. They can do this much in the same way individuals who are ignorant of their own gifts seek models to imitate in carrying out their roles as leaders, parents, or professionals. A major source for these models is academia, where theoretical models abound and are copied by those who are desperate for an organizational identity. Yet imitating an external model usually produces an organization inappropriately shaped for what it is doing.

Vision

The alternative to untried theoretical models is the development of a vision statement in collaboration with those gifted in facilitating such a process. A well-articulated vision statement portrays the best results that the organization can see itself bringing about as a consequence of its efforts. This picture not only gives direction, but becomes the glue that unifies the organization and differentiates it from all other organizations, including its competitors. The vision statement clarifies purpose and can be utilized to correct leaders who attempt to set inconsistent goals that would deflect the organization from its primary purpose.

Years ago, when Apple Computer said, "A computer in every home," it immediately differentiated itself from all other computer manufacturers. That vision took Apple products out of the limitation of being perceived of only as a business product and added a much larger market. Apple changed our culture and our way of thinking because of its vision. As soon as the vision was stated, every department of the company had to look at itself differently so that computer design at Apple was different from any other company. Apple sales became different. Every business activity became different. All of this took place when the company identified its vision and thereby described its own uniqueness. Churches, schools, and families all become better when they can move away from aping everyone else and articulate and confess who they are and how they are different.

Mission

No organization has the instinct, or the genius, for being anything other than what it is equipped to be through its people. When a Vision Statement (This is what we and our results should look like . . .) is translated into a Mission Statement (. . . therefore this is what we must do), it becomes increasingly clear whether the necessary resources are in place to achieve the stated goals. What kinds of leaders, what kinds of expertise, what kinds of systems, and what kinds of strategies are all implied by the Mission Statement as its goals are translated into plans. The style and the substance of how all this is done, then, emerges from the inherent nature of the organization rather than from some idealized, external model. That does not preclude the adaptation of any technique, process, or method developed elsewhere. Why reinvent that which has already proven itself? However, the determination of what preexisting methodology or system is appropriate for the organization is implied by a well-shaped Mission Statement.

CHANGES

Every organization is in a process of change, whether or not it intends to be. Change is the context in which all organizations exist. Changes can be ignored as haphazard occurrences, for which the organization is unprepared, or they can be managed. Managing change is key to keeping the organization at the cutting edge of its purposes. There are two opposing forces that confuse the process of managing change. One force is made up of those in the organization who are the Conservatives. They are the traditionalists, and they usually oppose change. Their combatants are the Innovators, Mavericks, and Developers, all devoted to bring about change.

There are a variety of types in each of the two camps. The Conservatives include those who have been in the organization for a long time and can tell stories of the company's history; those who don't know the stories but who temperamentally dislike change of any kind; and those who are gifted to maintain stability, order, and efficiency. The Change Agents are made up of persons ranging from those who simply like novelty and variety up to those who are genuinely creative. The two camps frequently operate like political parties, each group self-righteously working to dominate the organization. Both groups are usually present in every business, church, and school, and sometimes in families. Both are important resources in any organization. Wise leaders not only recognize their importance, but know how to manage the tension created by their mutual opposition.

If either side should win it would be a defeat, not merely for the opposing group, but for the entire organization. If the Conservatives win, new developments will cease and the organization will not remain on the cutting edge in its field of action. It will not be prepared for future changes, which in some cases will mean its eventual demise. If the Change Agents win, the organization will not know how to stay true to its own identity. Development and creative efforts will become haphazard, without the direction that organizational history affords. If the top leadership is a solo performance, without the balancing input of others, then the leader will tilt the organization toward one or the other party.

Conservatives prevent organizational amnesia, so decisions can be made in the context of previous experience. This eliminates the impulsive or erratic. Change Agents keep organizations alive and growing with new products, improved business processes, and fresh ideas. Every organization should value both its Change Agents and its Conservatives and deliberately use them as catalysts in each other's strategic planning sessions. The result is orderly, efficient growth and development.

UNWANTED CHANGES

People bring their gifts to organizations. These are precious resources. People also bring their needs to organizations. For example, people are mortals hoping for immortality, so they want their organizations to last forever. Organizations do not have that capacity. The Roman Empire was not able to sustain itself forever, and neither will the corner bookstore, IBM, or our alma mater. Leaders who fail to believe that every organization is mortal cannot see the signals indicating change, or perhaps that it is time to retrench or close shop. What should be a proactive process, with plans and strategies for termination, including transitioning clients and employees, ends up as a crisis. Too often we waste resources better used elsewhere in attempting to sustain organizations whose time is over. That is especially hard to realize for a nonprofit organization that once provided a viable service or ministry. Many ministries and service organizations attempt to maintain their institutional lives after the need for them is past, or after the visionary leader is gone. Their boards seem incapable of formally bringing to a close what already has ended. Their inclination is supported by the unrealistic assumption of almost every institution, the belief that it is destined for perpetuity.

ULTIMATE ALLEGIANCES

Organizations of all kinds can occupy an idolatrous position in the hearts of the people of which they are composed. No organization is meant for ultimate allegiance, yet human longing for meaning may find us substituting an organization for spiritual reality. The mission of the organization then becomes the mission of our lives, creating inordinate personal priorities. In the business world, this may convert us into supporters of policies and laws that assure our continued membership, irrespective of the needs of the organization and the unfair drain those policies may impose upon its resources and upon the wealth it returns to the economy. In nonprofit organizations it can have the effect of changing the focus from mission to institutional survival. Leaders should not feed this human tendency toward idolatry, even to enhance morale or esprit de corps.

SECURITY

Fear also makes its demands. The desire for security attaches us to our places of work like barnacles on a pier, making us willing to accumulate years and years of unfulfilled hours in labor we know does not fit us. Fear prevents us from abandoning what is clearly not good for us, so we end up mouthing the demand that we have a right to job security. We do so in the face of the astounding words of Jesus.

> Put away anxious thoughts about food and drink to keep you alive,
> and the clothes to cover your body. Surely life is more than food,
> the body more than clothes. Look the birds of the air; they do not
> sow and reap and store in barns, yet your heavenly Father feeds
> them. You are worth more than the birds! *(Matthew 6:25–34 NEB)*

This is not to diminish an organization's responsibilities to its workers, but none of us, regardless of the degree of authority we may have, or the level on which we may be working, should skirt around a confrontation with what Jesus Christ is addressing here. Many have never taken the risk Jesus portrays and wonder why they have but a vague sense of God's reality in their lives. From them we hear only faint stories of God's faithfulness rather than decisive declarations of victory. When the words from Matthew become experience, we will come to know something substantial of God's care for us, a divine concern we cannot otherwise apprehend. Simply put, genuine security cannot come from organizations. It comes only from God.

CHAPTER 12

―――――― ⌒⟋⟋⟋⟋⟍ ――――――

SELECTING
LEADERS

F illing leadership positions with those who have the appropriate gifts
should be one of the highest priorities of an organization. It is key
to the success of every human effort, but especially to the complex
activities of institutions. No organization can accomplish any more than
its leaders equip it to do. Therefore, the kind of thinking that is engaged
and the kind of selection process that is used to acquire leaders must be
exquisite. Here are some critical items to be considered.

JOB DESCRIPTIONS

We are deluded if we believe that a job description, as accurate as it
may be, is an insurance policy against mediocre performance. Nailing
down the detail of what is required in a job is only one part of the process. Appropriate selection requires the identification of those gifts that
will actually match what is in the job description. Giving authority to a
person who does not have the gifts to pull off what is needed assures
mediocrity. Giving authority to the person with the appropriate gifts and
experience can only end up with excellence.

LEVELS OF AUTHORITY

Determining a leader's gifts, training, and experience can help us estimate how high a level of authority for him might make sense for the future. This is especially valuable in the development of young leaders. For example, merely the factor of staying on top of information and data would be important for many of the high echelon positions of leadership, but that same level might also mean a reduction of the numbers of people being directly led. In many institutions, the degree of face-to-face leadership gets reduced the higher one climbs. That is fitting for some leaders and a misfit for others. Leaders do not fit just anywhere leadership is needed. They fit where their particular style of leadership is required.

SPECIFICS

The process of selecting leaders is where idealized definitions of leaders are incredibly dangerous to the organization. We need to know the specifics of what is to be accomplished, how it is to be done, and how long the gifts of a particular leader will be useful. Is an organization well served by retaining a leader who was acquired to reduce chaos to order, when order has been achieved—especially if the next phase requires development?

TAKE A NEW LOOK

Institutions do themselves a disservice by acquiring leaders in reaction to the last leader. One organization we know had a very powerful Influencing Leader who had no managerial abilities. The result was a great sense of purpose and direction, but much confusion about how to get to where they knew they should go. In reaction, they replaced the Influencing Leader with a Manager, who introduced considerable relief for the staff. He replaced all the confusion with order, procedures, and systems. However, the former clarity of mission eventually became dim. Morale and quality started to erode. The organization began to doubt its own validity, which, in turn, affected the constituency it served. Reactions and counter-reactions to this could have the organization on a pendulum moving back and forth over the years. The cure was to hire an Influencing President and back him up with an Influencing Manager, who mediated between the vision and the operation, the calling and the execution, the goals and the follow-up.

Leadership selection is not a matter of filling a job. It is a commit-ment to long-term strategy as embodied by the leader as he or she inter-faces in a complementary way with other leaders. The following compo-nents need to be covered in any institution where it is critical that the top leadership be visionary or developmental rather than managerial. Each component can be covered by one or more persons in whatever organi-zational structure will sustain excellent results.

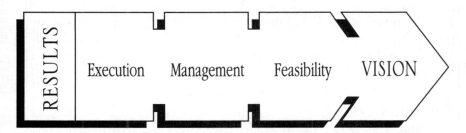

It should never be assumed that a permanent visionary should be at the helm of every organization. How much vision is needed? Some or-ganizations require a constant flow of visionary ideas, whereas others re-quire them sporadically. Rethinking the complementary cooperation of visionary, feasibility, and management functions of leadership is a door to the most effective organizational structures. Flexibility at the top of an organization is ideal for innovating such an interface but not likely to be attained if the president thinks in terms of power or control.

The feasibility component is sometimes covered by the Visionary Leader, but not often. Visionary and Developmental Leaders tend to be too optimistic in their assessment of what is feasible in terms of objec-tives, resources, and time schedules. For this reason they need to be open to (or a procedure should require) feasibility checks from a leader-ship team or a key manager or vice-president.

When it is clear what kind of leaders is required, the following questions become applicable. Attaining accurate answers can save much grief.

1
What critical results must the new leader obtain?
2
How will these results be attained?
3
What complementary leaders will be required?
4
How long will it take to attain the goals?
5
How will the results be measured?
6
What kind of leadership will then be required?
7
How will this procedure be monitored?

Question 6 implies that the organization needs certain kinds of leaders at each phase of its growth. These phases can move by quickly in a new organization but then slow down as maturity is gained. If it is known that the need for a particular kind of leader is going to be short-lived, the organization should contract such services accordingly, compensate to make the position very attractive, and take on the responsibility of supporting that leader in connecting to other opportunities at the appropriate time. Failure to agree to short-term or moderately short-term contracts will assure great pain for everyone concerned. It is easy to come to agreement prior to the hire and almost impossible once a leader has been in place for a period of time, even with leaders whose character or theology would suggest otherwise.

LEVELS

The popular idea that one should always climb as high as possible is dangerous. It has brought about misery in those leaders who believed it and acted on it. Too many did not know how to recognize the level they best fit so they could strategize a way to remain there. Too many others have assumed that only the top is the best. Reality demonstrates that it is only best for those for whom it fits.

What can make all this even more difficult is that not many organizations have a way to reward people who have prevented themselves from being promoted from a fitting level of leadership action to a misfit level. Forward-looking organizations need to plan how to offer career options that do not require climbing managerial ladders when such a climb makes no sense for an employee and therefore no sense for the organization.

KEY LEADERSHIP ERRORS

Each organization is prone to make typical mistakes based poor selection procedures or leadership misfit. Here are three examples.

Business: Lopsided Leadership

It is common in business corporations to see the top leadership come from the area of finance or business. The practice is so built into the culture of many companies that there seems to be no way to correct it. The people who have the power to make such changes are those who have come up the path we describe.

The result of this practice creates a hierarchy of top leaders who are often disconnected from many of the realities of the company below their level and who often become a remote class unto themselves. The kind of data in which they have an interest is available to them through the computer and is usually restricted to business matters. They are for the most part unaware of all the other remaining information, which is most of the information. ·

Those in this corporate leadership class tend to overestimate the accuracy of what they believe to be true about the company. They are cut off from most of the best advice available in the company by many below them who control the information, those who themselves have ambitions to join the upper levels. It has been remarkable to observe companies seeking the expertise of consultants to solve problems that could be easily solved by people already on their payroll, but of whose existence they remain unaware other than as names on organizational charts. Every organization needs to examine its key leadership to assure there is symbiosis between stabilizing functions and cutting edge advances.

Families: Idealized Job Description

The family is the primary organization of our society. It is the resource for all other organizations. If it does well, we all do well. The models for leadership have influenced our families to an unhappy degree. Many mothers and fathers are attempting to become the kind of parents that the books and magazine articles describe as the ideal. Churches tend to support this practice, adding the guilt of failing God to the guilt of failing the model.

Most of the principles we are presenting in this book fit the organization of the family. Parents need to discover the gifts they have and learn how to work in a complementary fashion with their spouses. Each parent is unique. That is how God made them, so we assume that is exactly how He intended it to be.

The prerequisite for being a good parent is being an authentic person. Children are learning how to become the individuals God made them to be and need to see how authentic individuals look and act. Do they see people trying to be somebody else, or do they see people who are free to be the persons God created them to be?

The child must know that he is a miracle; that since the beginning of the world there hasn't been, and until the end of the world there will not be, another child like him.

Pablo Casals

Children need to see parents as authentic and unique. Parents have an intense degree of influence in the lives of their children, so when parents are examples of healthy individualism, it becomes an indelible impression. At the same time, children need to see parents sacrificing their motivational interests and style for the sake of others, especially them. That teaches children how they sometimes need to relate to others. When they see the strong personalities of their parents adjusting themselves for the sake of others, it is a powerful demonstration. However, parents who are always conforming to some external model of parenting cannot display such power and therefore will deprive their children of a vivid illustration of what it means to relate to and love others.

There are two ways we love children. We give of our gifts. We also withhold our gifts so their gifts can be expressed. Our children could not initially select us as parents in the way that a company can select its leaders. However, our leadership should be so strongly *for* our children that they will emotionally select us as parents for the remainder of our lives. That is the most valuable leadership there is.

When God invents individuals, He paradoxically nurtures individuality in community. We cannot become ourselves by ourselves. Our children illustrate that as their uniqueness blooms in the context of family. A useful context for enhancing our families can be found in a community setting larger than a single family. Then several fathers and mothers can complement and support one another. In such a context, children see a variety of adult authorities relating to them and to each other. That provides a richer experience without the loss of the primary authority of their own parents. That is one of the benefits of small towns and small churches. But it is also a benefit that can be established by enlisting four or five couples into a small, supporting community that meets every so often.

For many years we experienced such a setting for our family and are aware of the rich benefits for children and adults alike. In our case, we brought together couples who were in highly individualistic professions and not attracted to large social events. That provided some commonality to the otherwise wide diversity. The setting was good for the children, who participated in the celebrations and the events in addition to observing the adult study and discussion times.

Churches: The Need for Leadership Diversity

The church sits on top of the largest inactive human resource in the world. Considering the nature of the church's mission, that is a disaster for the world. It isn't that church leaders have not been made aware of the critical need for equipping the saints to do the work of the ministry. There are many books on the subject. The basic problem is that, for the most part, pastors cannot do what is required. There are two reasons for this. One is that there is an inordinate number of controlling pastors in our churches through whom every decision must pass. They want their parishioners to be involved and active, but under their control. By this action they inadvertently present themselves as examples of leaders who believe they possess all the gifts. That is the only conclusion possible when one pastor's decisions are required for business, theology, education, plant management, committee selection, publicity, finance, church growth, and counseling. Such control alienates all those in the church who have careers based on those specialties and who could supply superior contributions in each. Such control alienates leaders, who feel they are not trusted because they are not trusted. Such control alienates creative people, whose gifts do not flourish in the context of control, conformity, and predictability. It keeps such churches from being at the cutting edge of anything.

For many reasons, the modern church has systematically kept creativity outside its doors. Without creative power to generate new approaches to every activity of the church, the church is forced to imitate the world. Instead of authentic worship, we end up with entertainment because that is what the world is good at. Instead of learning how to be led by the Holy Spirit, we end up with corporate strategies. Instead of spiritual power, we end up with political power. Our failure to appreciate and orchestrate all the gifts of the body as taught by the apostle Paul is a profound but largely unrecognized tragedy. Some of the corporate clients we deal with professionally know more about empowering people than the organization whose Scriptures are the source for the principles of empowerment. The church has paid dearly for its inadequate perceptions of leadership.

The second reason the laity are not in the action is because it requires management gifts to involve people. People need to be recruited to fulfill responsibilities that fit their gifts. They need to be empowered and managed appropriately. Pastors are rarely gifted or equipped to do this, nor should they. The best solution is to find parishioners who have the gifts to do the recruiting and managing. There are two problems here. One is that many churches have little appreciation for the gifts of the manager. It appears too businesslike for them. It doesn't sound very spiritual. In actuality, managers are defined as individuals who have the gifts to work through people to get results. We know managing is a set of gifts that God created because no one else can design human gifts.

However, there is good news. We have been working for several years in two churches which have been pleased to be laboratories for us. One is an average-sized church in New England. The other is a large church in Texas. They have different cultures and different leaders, yet with all the differences, we have been able to develop the same results. Both churches have effectively tapped the laity to a degree previously not thought possible. Both churches have installed a process of identifying, developing, and placing leaders that has delighted the leaders and the churches. All of this preserves the particular vision each church has of its unique position in its respective community. We now have evidence that it can be done.

The last point to be made is in regard to pastors. The last time we researched our files to see how pastors are gifted to accomplish their responsibilities, we were refreshed once again with the display of endless variety. God does not merely supply us with pastors. He supplies us with pastors who can fit every kind of opportunity that exists in churches, no matter where those churches may be, or what condition in which they may find themselves. There are pastors who can fit any church, but probably for a particular period of time depending on the phase of growth in which the church body finds itself. The life of a church requires different leaders at different times. The gifts of a pastor requires certain conditions every time. Our prayers and selection procedures should reflect these realities.

BEING SELECTED

The search for, and selection of a leader involves more than those who are on the hunt for the candidate. It calls for the response of a candidate to the opportunity. When any organization tells someone that he or she is the person for whom it has been seeking, that can stir up many contravening feelings. Although it is always a delight to be the object of others' enthusiasm, it also can be dangerous to our well-being. We may be tempted to take on that which will deflect us from what we understand we are meant to do. Assuming that the proffered opportunity fits our gifts and degree of experience, there still remains the question of its fitting our destiny.

The word *destiny* may be too strong a word for some readers. If that is the case, use a word that conveys the sense of purpose that is yours, that which interfaces with the sovereignty of God in creating you. It is not uncommon for a leader to locate a place within himself where responsibilities as a leader not only connect with gifts, but also with a realization of personal "rightness," of being where one belongs. It may be in an unobtrusive role, or it may involve fame. It may be changing the lives of small children, or it may be changing international affairs. Regardless of the context, only in that interior place is one's vision of grandeur perceived. Attempts to conjure up such a vision based on transient worldly values cannot be sustained beyond the world that imparted those values. We are made for something better. It includes and goes beyond the world as we now know it. The grandest vision is when our perceptions about our lives, careers, and relationships are informed by an understanding of the infinite God, who created finite humans and is moving them through the kingdoms of time toward the New Kingdom. That is what we must keep our eyes upon. That is what imparts meaning to this moment and to each moment.

We realize that when a leader looks at a particular opportunity, there are many practical considerations that may involve family, relocation, and compensation. All that must be carefully thought through. However, we suggest that the best decisions engage the harmony of the immediate with the reality of the big picture. Such a view can help clarify the rightness of any particular leadership opportunity. The grand view is also the source of bullish energy for what lies ahead in any situation.

CHAPTER 13

HIGH HOPES

The energy of leadership comes from the quality of a leader's gifts, skills, character, and relationship with God. But there is an additional source, and that is the vitality, the élan, of the society in which the leader lives. An optimistic and creative society stimulates its leaders toward magnificent accomplishments, which, in turn, inspires even greater levels of vigorous leadership. In contrast, timid societies are limited by small concepts, fear of circumstances, and pessimism. In such a milieu there appears to be no alternative but decline, a situation that can only be reversed by leaders who are grasped by a new vision.

Our age needs leaders on all levels, in all fields of endeavor, not only to sustain progress, but also to generate optimism for future growth and advance. When optimism cannot be derived from the current state of affairs, we must look elsewhere for inspiration. For this reason, the objective of this last chapter is to connect our considerations about leadership to the largest organizations. By this we mean civilizations, which must be dealt with in terms of centuries and epochs. Although each of us can act only in the present moment, the more we understand from where it all has come to where it is going, the better informed will be our actions. The placement of one brick makes much more sense when we behold the entire building.

Since God is the author of the whole drama of human existence, some understanding of His action throughout history and upon our future adds zest to the living of our lives. But more than that, the larger perspective grants to the leader the motivation to enter his or her proper place of leadership with confidence. Our moments may be fleeting, but the entire history of mankind is made up of those fragments of action by individual people. We ought not to devalue the treasure of time and energy each of us has been given. Their value is measured by God, not by aeons. What God intends to ultimately accomplish is reason to give us high hopes regardless of the state of society in which we now live.

OPTIMISM

The driving force of Western civilization over the centuries has been rooted in biblical assumptions. Technical development, the age of exploration, and the spirit of progress itself are characteristically Western and founded upon the optimism of a Judeo-Christian worldview. This has been illustrated by the Western expectation of continual advancement in contrast to the fixed, unvarying traditions of Asian civilizations. Though the clarity of this example has been muddied for the contemporary viewer by the current westernization of Asia, history makes clear that the Western spirit made it more likely for the Europeans to discover and investigate China than the other way around. For good or ill, the West is characteristically inspired by opportunities for expansion, exploration, and discovery. This is what generated the industrial revolution in Europe, Britain, and the United States, an impossibility in traditional Asia. It has been said that Japan could only bring about its own industrial revolution after the West provided the model and only after a severe erosion of its ancient religious traditions, which had previously held such modernization at bay.

That is not to say that Asian countries did not develop. That would be absurd. China's culture, for example, rooted as it was in prehistory, had to develop in order to become a civilization. All civilizations develop and grow. Here, however, we refer to the character of Asian civilizations. That character was not a progressive, lineal advance forward as in the West. Development in China was more like the enhancement of an ever-revolving horizontal wheel, once primitive and now beautifully complex in its circular movement. In contrast, for the West, the metaphor of a wheel could only work if it were vertical and attached to a vehicle going somewhere. Buddhism, for example, easily adapted by China, rejected the material and the sensory for the immaterial. This is in stark contrast to the foundational beliefs of Western civilization, where God states that creation in all its concreteness and vitality is good, and where the Son of God actually takes on flesh and is described in the New Testament as one who came eating and drinking.

Another vivid picture of Judeo-Christian dynamism can be seen when Western civilization is compared to Egyptian civilization's three thousand years of the same cultural expression. Although the average college student is not likely to differentiate between Old Kingdom figurative sculpture and that of the Late Dynastic period, the average college student immediately recognizes Egyptian sculpture regardless of where it appears on the historical time line. That is because there was intense stylistic consistency in Egypt for three centuries. In comparison, in a time period little more than half the history of Egypt, Europe, born in the Middle Ages, goes through the Romanesque and Gothic periods, the entire Renaissance, the Reformation, the Age of Reason, followed by what has been called the Age of Enlightenment, the Industrial Revolution, the colonization of the Americas, and the entry into the Modern era. Since the foundational beliefs of a people determine the style of its culture, we can state that the propulsive power for so much change in the West was initiated by its biblical presuppositions. In contrast, the consistency of Egyptian culture was rooted in a long-lasting preoccupation with death, though not death as the West perceives it.

What are the biblical assumptions, and why are they important to the study of leadership?

So God created man in his own image, in the image of God he created him; male and female he created them. God blessed them, and said to them, "Be fruitful and increase, fill the earth and subdue it, rule over the fish of the sea, the birds of heaven, and every living thing that moves upon the earth." *(Genesis 1:27–28 NEB)*

Be fruitful.
Reproduce.
Produce.
Subdue.
Rule.

All are active, even aggressive words requiring initiative and effort by mankind. The foundation of civilization, with all its magnificence and wonder, begins here. Whether we scan vast fields of grain harvested by great mechanical harvesters, or bridges suspending grand highways over rivers, or splendid buildings, or computers, or brilliant poetry, or moon-bound rockets, we see their beginnings in the commands of God at the dawn of historic time. At any point in civilization's advance there have been those who wondered how it could be possible to go any further. They surely were not leaders. They were the pessimists, who forgot the commands of God and doubted the existence of the resources to accomplish the next phase in fulfilling those commands. Adam and Eve probably could not have imagined the extent and the amazing variety of resources already under their feet, enabling the eventual manufacture and development of every device and tool of civilization both functional and aesthetic. The implication of God's commands in Genesis is that there are always resources at hand, intellectual and material, to solve whatever problems we have and to advance further in our organizations and our civilizations than previous generations could imagine. Thousands of years of human progress affirm it.

It is this source of Western optimism that today's leaders need to better understand in order to move confidently into whatever arena of activity they find themselves. Why? Because, although Western optimism has inspired great civilizations in the past and generated the American constitution, we all know that the Western hope of uninterrupted progress has never been reality. Progress, yes, but not unbroken progress. Though Adam and Eve were called to establish civilization, they introduced a stumbling block to progress. They attempted to rid themselves of God's external authority in accomplishing their goals, in favor of self-sufficiency. All Adam's descendants, including you and me, have duplicated his trust in the illusion of self-sufficient knowledge rather than knowledge from, and obedience to, God. As a result, each achievement of man has to be wrested from the earth by sweat and laborious effort.

In addition, too often the sweetest achievements of our work are spoiled by greed. So repeated battles within ourselves and against barbarism without, have been necessary to retain the magnificence of Western achievement. These battles have required the presence of political leaders, churchmen, scientists, writers, artists, and businessmen—all tempted to retain the myopia of their own limited arena of activity or body of knowledge, but many of whom took up the fight. These battles continue to be fought in every area of human industry in our complex civilization. If we do not fight them, our civilization will fall just as easily as when a mere fifteen thousand barbarians in A.D. 406 began the dismantling of the colossal Roman Empire and in four years completed the job by sacking Rome. Who, then, could have imagined such an event?

Western optimism, however, is twofold: convictions about progress, and confidence in redemption when progress gets derailed. God acts redemptively in history on the one hand to save individuals who become derailed. This is personal salvation through the crucifixion and resurrection of Jesus Christ. On the other hand, God works redemptively in our history to overcome hurdles to progress and productivity. That was the principle laid down by God at the dedication of the temple by King Solomon in Jerusalem.

> If my people, which are called by my name, shall humble
> themselves, and pray, and seek my face, and turn from their wicked
> ways: then I will hear from heaven, and will forgive their sin, and
> will heal their land. *(2 Chronicles 7:14 KJV)*

How does He do this? He not only blesses climactically, He imparts abilities and gifts to mankind and can set us free to use them. The presence of problem solvers, managers, and strategists in our organizations is a gift from God. They are there to enhance our fruitfulness and move us forward. If we perceive this, we can better understand the severity of judgment for the person in the famous story of the talents in Matthew 25 who failed to be productive. In that chapter, Jesus describes the reaction of a man to a servant who buried money entrusted to him rather than investing it. "Fling the useless servant out into the dark, the place of wailing and grinding of teeth" (v. 30 NEB) is fierce punishment for not advancing business, but it does jar us into realizing something of the harvest God intends to gather in history and in heaven.

So, when we ask, "Who could have imagined the fall of Rome?" we can go further and ask a question implying the inevitability of the redemptive: "Standing on the ruins of the Roman Empire, surrounded by the barbarians, who could have imagined the glory of medieval civilization soaring out of the ashes of Rome?" Man's ego-centered failures and sin are always countered by the redemptive acts of God. He always wins! That is inevitable, and it is the foundation of long-term optimism, the driving force of past Western achievement. Even when we write our tragedies, we do so realizing that ultimately, from God's perspective, there is no tragedy. Consider how King David pleads with God to preserve him from his enemies and from the oppression of the wicked, but ends with this wonderful conclusion:

> As for me, I will behold thy face in righteousness: I shall be satisfied,
> when I awake, with thy likeness. *(Psalm 17:15 KJV)*

This is why the Judeo-Christian perspective has no choice but that of optimism. Leadership driven by such a perspective is full of substantial hope even when the leader is overwhelmed by opposition. We live in a time when the West is full of doubt and timidity and in need of leaders with vision, but it cannot be *any vision*. Vision is viable only to the degree it is rooted in the truths of responsible stewardship found in Genesis. Regardless of the place the leader occupies in history, be it high or be it low, the good news is that God is up to something. What a joy it is to participate.

CONCLUSIONS

1. People are meant to see themselves as the crown of creation with the earth simultaneously existing as a work of pleasure by and for God and as a stage of action for man. The book of Genesis clearly positions man as the key player in the process of ordering the world. We are to operate with the assumption that God has provided the resources for whatever it is appropriate for mankind to accomplish. Men and women are to be stewards of the beauty God created while being developers of its resources. Good stewardship requires the suitable use of land and people. Leaders are to work in harmony with the prior claim God has on any activity of mankind.

2. Leaders are to operate upon a foundation of optimism, realizing that God Himself infuses meaning into all we do and that He will bring about ultimate good. This optimism is based upon God's sovereignty rather than man's cleverness. It recognizes the reality of the fallen nature of man, and so is not surprised at failure or the presence of evil. It also recognizes the reality of redemption and its sure goal of ultimate success, even when there is an absence of immediate success.

3. Leaders are to be suspicious of their own knowledge because it is always fragmented and prone to be self-centered. This marks the vast difference between self-confidence based upon an inordinate trust in man's abilities and that founded upon an individual's and a community's relationship with God.

4. The Bible always connects the acts of individuals to the sweep of history. We diminish ourselves when we allow the relative shortness of our lives and action to be overwhelmed by the vast stretch of mankind's history. We repeat that which was stated earlier: it is who God is shaping us into as we do our work that is of great significance. Though the amount of time varies for each of us, all we need is just enough time for God to sculpt our character. All our individual characters are being shaped by God into one grand story with the most splendid denouement imaginable.

*Dear friends, now we are children of God,
and what we will be has not yet been made known.
But we know that when he appears, we shall be like him,
for we shall see him as he is.*

1 John 3:2 NIV